A Call to Family Reformation

*Restoring the Soul of America
One Home at a Time*

Dennis Rainey

FamilyLife is a division of Campus Crusade for Christ, Inc., an evangelical Christian organization founded in 1951 by Bill Bright. FamilyLife started in 1976 to help fulfill the Great Commission by strengthening marriages and families and then equipping them to go to the world with the gospel of Jesus Christ. Our FamilyLife Conferences are held in many cities throughout the United States. To obtain information on FamilyLife, either write or call us at the address listed below.

Verses are from the New American Standard Bible. Copyright © 1960, 1962, 1963, 1971, 1972, 1973, 1975, 1977 by the Lockman Foundation. Used by permission.

Flower bloom on the cover—copyright © 1994 PhotoDisc, Inc.

A Call to Family Reformation
Copyright 1996 by Dennis Rainey
ISBN 1-57229-029-3

FamilyLife
P.O. Box 23840
Little Rock, AR 72221-3840
(501) 223-8663
1-800-999-8663

http://www.familylife-ccc.org

Dedication

*T*his book is dedicated to the men and women whose
lives are being spent in the cause of Family Reformation.
It is my privilege to work with you!

Merle and Lynn Engle

Don and Suzanne Dudgeon

Bob and Mary Ann Lepine

Roger and Barbara Craft

Dave and Diana Daggett

Mark and Lisa Schatzman

Jeff and Brenda Schulte

Lloyd and Lisa Shadrach

Ken and Nook Tuttle

Blair and Debbye Wright

Jerry and Sheryl Wunder

Contents

Acknowledgements

*N*o book that I have written has ever been more challenging. Perhaps this project has been more difficult because the message is so weighty, and so important to so many. But my task was lightened by a battalion of committed warriors for the family. These frontline, battle-seasoned veterans have served with me in more than one spiritual skirmish. All deserve more thanks and appreciation than I could possibly express. But here goes...

Rich Campbell is one patient and faithful man who was sent by God for such a time as this. Really. I mean it. Your long hours, advice, gifted writing, and commitment are deeply appreciated. Thanks for stepping into a minefield and expending your life for a Family Reformation. I'd still be writing 8,000 word chapters and working on this beast if you hadn't joined the cause!!!! Thanks.

And to Dave Boehi, a veteran of many of these "book birthings," goes another long and loud set of kudos. *Bo knows books.* And editing. And logic. And my writing style. Thank you for rescuing Rich and me from the impossible job of editing. You've saved my life before and now you've done it again. I'm thrilled God has rewarded your years here at FamilyLife with the magazine *Real FamilyLife*. Thank you. Thank you.

Merle Engle is a servant-leader who made this book possible by managing the 200-plus staff here at FamilyLife. You have fought budget wars, battled fatigue brought on by long meetings, suffered a mild heart attack (hastened, no doubt, by your relationship with me!), and anguished over personnel problems. Thank you for taking on the unending challenge of computers, endeavoring to train us, coaching us in excellence, and exhorting us to read the Bible and pray more. Merle Engle—you are one of a kind! Your legacy is, and will be, great.

Jeff Schulte, Bob Lepine, and Lloyd Shadrach—the three of you deserve a medal for the philosophical and strategic edge you brought to the concept of Family Reformation. You men took the mandate and made it work. There would be no book without you. None!

To Mary Larmoyeux (the captain of the troops), Sharon Hill, Kathy Horton, Matt Burns, and Fran Taylor I offer up incredible thanks for researching, editing, juggling the details, and running an office in my absence. Awesome!

Kevin Hartman and Blair Wright are true leaders in the fight for the family and in the production of this book. Thank you for caring about the future of families, and for being "difference-makers" in tens of thousands of lives through materials like this one.

Chuck Bostwick, you took the challenge on the cover design and surprised no one! Everything you do is superb! There aren't enough courageous men today, but you are one of them. Well done! Great job, too, on the layout of the rest of the book.

Jeff Lord, you continue to grow while managing a very tough job. Thank you for your commitment to details over the years, details that generally go unnoticed unless there's a mistake. Thanks also for your commitment to excellence, and for serving with a willing spirit.

Julie Denker is once again a lifesaver in editing and proofing. Additional thanks go to Dan Butkowski, Anne Wooten, Sandy Harris, and Betty Dillon for the quality work you did on this book, and on all the other projects I have sent your way.

Rob and Laurie Kopf, this ministry would be in big trouble at the distribution center if you hadn't come along and bailed us out. You both make all of us at FamilyLife proud by your sacrificial service to folks who order our books and resources.

Tonda Nations, your initial work on the "Family Reformation" radio broadcast helped fuel my creativity. Exponential thanks. Tom Clagett, your research is invaluable and helped to shape the strategy of this book. Thanks to both of you for your "behind the scenes," but all-important work.

Bill Howard, your studious, year-long contribution to the *Family Manifesto* will never be forgotten. Thank you. Beth Greenway, Mary Pierce, and Bill Etter all deserve hearty thanks as well for your eleventh-hour editing contributions.

To Samuel, Rebecca, Deborah, and Laura, thank you for allowing me to come home a little later in the midst of this assignment. You are the best kids in the world. And to my two collegians, Ashley and Benjamin, I just want to say thanks for understanding why I couldn't come visit you at school during the writing of this book. It's been fun to have you back home recently. I love all six of you more than you'll ever know. You make me a proud papa! And when you get married, be sure you walk in the truth and love God with a whole heart—and challenge your generation to continue the Family Reformation.

And once again, I must turn and say thanks to my wife, Barbara, my friend and companion for life. Thank you for all the healthy food that kept me going in the midst of this book. I love you and appreciate you for being an awesome mother and an even better wife. I'd marry you all over again—ten times out of ten. And, yes, I'll lose ten pounds, now that the book is done. I love you.

And finally, a heartfelt thank you to the hundreds of FamilyLife staff and the thousands of volunteers across the country and around the world who are igniting the flame of a Family Reformation!

A Note to Our Readers

*A*s writers, we face a dilemma. The English language does not contain a one-word equivalent for "he or she," yet we find it cumbersome to repeatedly refer to your mate or child as "he or she." Therefore, for the sake of readability, we generally will refer to your mate or child as "he."

The Silent Stirrings of Reformation

The only real revolutions are those that change the mind and the heart, and the only real revolutionaries are the sage and the saint.

—Will and Ariel Durant

Chapter One

*L*ight snow fell on the cobblestone streets of
Wittenberg, Germany, as a middle-aged man,
dressed in the garb of an Augustinian monk, trudged slowly
across the university grounds and made his way home for the
evening. Gravel crunched on the well-worn path beneath his
feet; the wind, blustery and unrelenting, pricked at the
exposed flesh on his face.

Everything about the man's appearance and demeanor
hinted at his growing sense of despair. A scowl cut deeply
into his forehead, and his hands, which often swung freely in
rhythm with his step, were buried inside the lining of his
coat. But the most telling characteristic of all was the simple
fact that he was alone.

Jovial, boisterous, and witty, Martin Luther was
rarely alone.

On most nights, Luther made the half-mile journey
from the classroom to the cloister in the company of
students. A professor of theology, he delighted in the cama-
raderie of friends and the repartee of theological debate.
Since his arrival at Wittenberg in April 1511, Luther had
become a social and spiritual magnet. Students devoured his
classes and sought out his opinion on a wide array of theological issues. Always accessible, Martin Luther did some of
his best teaching at night, on the journey home. It was not
uncommon to observe the professor strolling leisurely with a

flock of adoring disciples in tow. The residents of Wittenberg had grown accustomed to seeing Luther, surrounded by a group of eager students, gesturing dramatically as he reinforced a theological point.

And Martin wasn't afraid to buttress his views with a touch of bravado. On one occasion, to the sheer delight of his late-night audience, Luther had hurled his cap into the Elbe River to demonstrate his contempt for the doctrine of papal infallibility. On another, he opened his Latin Bible, the Vulgate, and tore out the books of the Apocrypha, charging that they didn't belong in Scripture. For these and other mischievous deeds, Martin Luther was viewed as a renegade by his students. He always attracted a crowd and relished the opportunity of shaping young minds.

But tonight there would be no company and no conversations. And that was just the way he wanted it.

The dirt path came to a dead end. Pausing to readjust his cap—which the students had purchased to replace the one he had pitched into the river—Luther veered to the right and continued the trek home. He was now on the main road, at the northeastern edge of Wittenberg. Shadows lay across the street, devouring passersby and, some nights, concealing an occasional hoodlum or thief.

But unlike the sedate surroundings of the university, the village was bustling with activity. All around him, preparations were under way for All Saints' Day. Shopkeepers labored long into the night, stocking shelves to accommodate the influx of visitors from the countryside. Carnival tents were being erected in the town square. Excited bands of young people ran to and fro, ignoring the darkness and anticipating the celebration that was only two days away.

The Silent Stirrings of Reformation

All Saints' Day, held annually on November 1, commemorated the lives of great saints. Though it provided many people with an excuse to get drunk, the holiday still retained a strong religious undercurrent. On November 1, emissaries of Pope Leo X would openly display the bones and relics of dead saints and peddle religious dispensations called "indulgences." For a financial contribution, a sinner could purchase an indulgence and reduce the sentence—for himself and others—in purgatory.

This practice, which, in Luther's mind, constituted a violation of Scripture, would commence in two days. For months, Martin Luther had been framing a theological response against the sale of indulgences. He had conceived a daring plan to proclaim his opposition. Tomorrow, Luther intended to march to the castle church, where indulgences had been sold in years past, and nail his list of protests to the church door.

The risks were enormous. He knew this seeming act of defiance could cost him his professorship: Profits from the sale of indulgences financed the very institution for which he labored. He also knew that the Roman Church had little patience for dissenters. He could expect to elicit its wrath.

Assailed by these fears and doubts, Luther trudged wearily onward; past the shops, past the tents and the children, through the bustling village of Wittenberg. At the edge of town, he ascended a flight of stairs, leaned into the oak door of his small room, and kindled a fire to chase away the cold.

Luther sat in the flickering light of the fire, praying for strength but feeling only dread. His life would be changed, irrevocably, tomorrow. He glanced at the document lying on the table before him. *Throw it into the fire,* the voice of doubt whispered in his ear. Martin reached for the parchment; he was torn between self-preservation and righteous indignation. "Maybe I'm just a fool," he thought to himself. "Am I the only one troubled by this affront to God?"

Slowly, reflectively, Martin Luther began to re-read the document he had taken months to compose. As he did, a spirit of resolve stirred within his breast. He determined to consummate the ordeal, regardless of the personal cost. Late into the night, Luther sat alone in his room. In the presence of an almighty God, he grew stronger; his fears abated. But this assurance didn't come until well past midnight.

For Martin Luther, professor of theology at the University of Wittenberg, the evening of October 30, 1517, would prove to be one of the longest nights of his life.

Debi Godsey was also contemplating an audacious act, but it probably wouldn't alter the course of Western civilization. In fact, other than a few friends and family members, no one would notice (or even care), that she was dead. After all, how many people actually read the obituary column in the *Milwaukee Journal*?

For months, Debi had been planning her suicide. The 33-year-old blonde-haired, blue-eyed bartender just wanted to escape her pain. "I wasn't afraid of going to hell," she said. "I had already lived through hell for most of my life."

From the beginning, Debi knew the sting of rejection and the reproach of shame. Her mother divorced Debi's father during Debi's teenage years; her dad took up temporary residence in a Georgia jail. Throughout her adolescent years, Debi rarely saw her father, and after he jumped bail all contact ceased for four years.

In 1978, at the age of 22, Debi learned that her dad was living in Wisconsin. Seeking a new start, she left the South and relocated in the Dairy State. Married, separated, and pregnant at the time, Debi moved in with her father. After her daughter Carla was born, Debi and her husband reunited. But when Carla was only 16 months old, the couple divorced.

Over the next ten years, Debi went from one failed relationship to another. She packed a handgun to protect herself against the low-life creatures who frequented the bars where she worked. She used drugs and alcohol religiously. There was an abusive relationship that scarred her body and damaged her psyche. There was also an abortion. Her second marriage, begun in 1984, would soon be terminated by the courts.

For Debi, the 1990s began just as pitifully as the previous decade had ended. Resolved to close the curtain on a failed life, she rehearsed and planned the details of her own death. Debi settled on a day: October 29,1990. That was the day her divorce would be finalized.

The owner of a VT-1100 Shadow motorcycle, Debi intended to drive her bike head-on into a large truck at 80 miles an hour. It was now mid-October. The day of deliverance was two weeks away.

She wondered if she could wait that long.

Hours passed. The fire faded. A mouse scurried across the hardwood floor of Luther's spartan dwelling place. It paused momentarily, picking at stale crumbs under the table, and then scampered along the wall before disappearing into the darkness. The rodent's tiny claws scratched the floor and roused Martin from his preoccupation.

"Tetzel, is that you?" inquired Luther, with a note of glee in his voice.

The gloom of early evening had given way to the joy of resolution.

Luther rose from his chair, placed the document on the seat behind him, and laughed out loud. He tossed a log on the fire and rubbed his hands over the expanding flame. Dubbing his late-night visitor "Tetzel" was, in Luther's mind, a stroke of genius, and provided him with a never-ending source of merriment. But it also made him angry. To Martin, the similarity between Tetzel the mouse and Tetzel the priest was obvious. Both were shrewd thieves. Tetzel the mouse regularly invaded Luther's cupboard, stealing his meager ration of foodstuffs. John Tetzel the priest was also a thief, of the more repulsive variety.

An emissary for the Pope, Tetzel dispensed indulgences among the naive citizens of Germany. Forbidden to enter Saxony for political reasons, Tetzel hawked his wares just across the border. The members of Luther's parish traveled regularly over the border to buy what they thought were spiritual favors from God: a complete remission of sins and relief from the pains of purgatory.

A vendor *par excellence*, Tetzel even coined a jingle that was particularly offensive to Luther. When he entered a village amid the pomp of a solemn procession, Tetzel would cry out: "As soon as the coin in the coffer rings, the soul from purgatory springs!"

Martin had learned to tolerate the mouse, but he could never abide an offensive Dominican priest who peddled supernatural dispensations.

Anger surged in Luther's veins. The night was now short. There were only a few more hours until daylight. Not even enough time to sleep. Martin walked over to his bed, grabbed a blanket, and returned to his place in front of the fire. He stretched the woolen quilt over his medium-sized frame, leaned back in his chair, and prayed that when the sun rose tomorrow, he would still have the courage to confront the darkness.

In Debi's mind, Jim Godsey was a chief cause of her unrelenting sorrow. The couple met in 1981 when Debi was tending bar at Captain Jack's West in Pewaukee, Wis. Like most of the regulars, Jim came in every night and got drunk. Seeking a companion to ease his loneliness, he immediately latched on to Debi.

"Jim was a happy drunk," says Debi. "He was fun to be with." In time, the happy-go-lucky romantic won over Debi's affections. Jim would hang around and rub her aching feet at the end of her shift. A one-night stand turned into a live-in relationship. But almost immediately there were problems.

"I'd kick him out," she recalls, "and he would move right back in. I couldn't get rid of him."

Jim was unemployed throughout the first year of their

relationship. Debi issued an ultimatum: find a job or get out. In 1983, he found work at a paper mill in Milwaukee. The following year, on August 11, they were married. Jim adopted Debi's daughter; Carla took Jim's last name.

But nothing changed.

Debi continued to tend bar while Jim, an alcoholic since high school, drank constantly. They did drugs. And fought incessantly. Debi had a number of extra-marital affairs.

Six years passed. In January of 1990, by common consent, the Godseys filed for divorce. Debi moved out in June and began living with her next boyfriend. Comatose, lifeless, and ready for burial, the Godseys' marriage awaited only the final verdict of a merciful judge.

The divorce was supposed to be finalized on June 10, but the judge went on vacation. The court date was rescheduled for July. But this created another delay. To repair the huge machines at the paper mill where Jim worked, the company shut down for two weeks in July. As a mechanic, Jim's schedule was doubled, from 40 to 80 hours a week. The shutdown coincided with the court date, which was rescheduled, again, for October 29.

Debi grew more and more despondent with each postponement. She devoured tranquilizers. Her doctor drew up paperwork to commit her to the St. Michael's psychiatric care unit. Debi talked him out of it. Despair pressed evermore firmly against her broken will.

In mid-August 1990, Debi was driving down the freeway; she was exasperated and forlorn. She shook her fist at God and cried out: "If there is a God, then I need answers!"

But none came.

A day went by.

Then a week.

The despair mounted. Debi saw no hope for her life, and suicide became the only reasonable alternative. The date was set. Her resolution grew stronger with each passing day. On October 29, Debi would finally be free from Jim.

And free from all the pain.

One eminent historian has concluded: "If we judge greatness by influence...we may rank Luther with Copernicus, Voltaire, and Darwin as the most powerful personalities in the modern world."[1] And so it is. But on the morning of October 31, 1517, as the sun burst through the single window of his small flat in Wittenberg, Germany, Martin Luther wasn't thinking about greatness or influence or the judgment of history. In his mind, he was nothing more than a simple Augustinian monk who was committed to the truths of Scripture. And those truths—at least in regard to the sale of indulgences—had been violated. He could no longer remain silent.

Martin sat listlessly for a moment and then perched himself upright in his chair. A pool of sunlight lay motionless in the center of the room. The doubts of the previous night were gone; they had been displaced by the certainty of conviction.

Luther resolved to act quickly. He rose to his feet, stretched his arms horizontally, and ran his fingers through his wavy black hair. Hurriedly, he stepped into his coat and picked up a hammer and a single nail lying at the base of the fireplace.

A Call to Family Reformation

As Martin glanced at the cold ashes, his mind raced ahead to his destination: the door. Luther knew that the door of the castle church in Wittenberg had two functions. One was to keep the cold German winter out of the sanctuary; the other was to disseminate information. Since the town had no newspapers, the church door served as a conduit for communication, dialogue, and debate—a sort of medieval bulletin board. For his convictions to influence others, Luther knew that he needed to post his document for all to read—on that door.

Out *his* door and down the stairs he went, retracing his journey from the previous evening. His pace was brisk and he glided over the rough surface of the deserted street. At the opposite end of town, Martin Luther mounted the steps of the castle church. A few early-morning worshippers glanced in his direction but said nothing.

Standing squarely in front of the massive door, Luther cradled the document in his left hand. He then reached into his coat pocket for the tools of revolution. Using the base of his left hand to secure the parchment against the door, Luther raised the hammer aloft, and struck the piece of rusty metal. It penetrated the paper and the wood, and the sharp CRACK echoed down the lonely streets of Wittenberg. Four more blows finished the job.

Martin Luther turned his back to the church and headed home. As he strolled amiably in the bright sunlight, pleased with his obedience, Luther had no idea how much his life would soon be transformed. Within months, he would become the talk of Germany. In a few years, he would be hunted by papal representatives as an enemy of the Holy Roman Church. This one act of obedience, like few others in human history, would alter the course of western civilization.

The Protestant Reformation had begun.[2]

The telephone rang in Debi's trailer. It startled her. She was living with her boyfriend just outside of Milwaukee and didn't receive many calls. Only a few friends knew her phone number. Debi picked up the receiver and was surprised to hear Mark's voice.

Mark was an old drinking buddy who used to party with Jim and Debi during the "good old days." "Can I take you to lunch?" he asked. "I'd really like to talk to you." Debi consented. They made plans to see one another the next week, the last week in August.

Over lunch, Mark said some things that surprised Debi. She had heard that Mark had quit the party scene and was no longer drinking. He confirmed this. Mark also mentioned that he and his wife Patty had attended a marriage conference and had discovered the secret to a happy, exciting marriage.

He added that another conference was going to be held the middle of October and encouraged Debi to attend. "When Mark said that," Debi recalls, "the hair stood up on the back of my neck. I was determined to get out of my marriage, and the last thing I wanted to do was attend a marriage conference."

But Mark was persistent. And shrewd as a serpent. "Debi," he asked, "if I can get Jim to go, will you go too?" Convinced that Jim would never agree to this—not in a million years—she relented. To get Mark off of her back,

Debi agreed to go, but only if Jim said yes.

A week later, Mark took Jim to dinner. He mentioned the marriage conference. Jim's response was emphatic: "No way!" Knowing about Debi's tentative consent, Mark said, "Jim, if I can get Debi to go, will you go too?" Still Jim hesitated. But after much coercion, Jim agreed to attend—if Debi would too.

A registration form was filled out; a check was mailed in. And incredibly, on October 19, 1990, Jim and Debi Godsey found themselves in the most unlikely of places: the FamilyLife Marriage Conference at the Marriott Hotel in Brookfield, Wis.

I happened to be one of the speakers that weekend.

The alienated couple sat together, cold and distant, during the sessions on Friday night. The other conference speaker, Stu Weber, detailed the five steps in the death of a marriage. Back in their hotel room later that evening, Debi blurted out, "Jim, there are five steps in the death of a marriage; we're at step number six!" Grasping at straws, Jim responded, "Debi, if the speakers know the way down, then they also must know the way back."

Throughout the next day, Stu Weber and I took turns introducing the couples to God's blueprint for a healthy marriage. After the final session Saturday afternoon, Debi approached me. She looked exhausted. She asked me to pray for her. And then she added, "Dennis, in nine days my marriage and my life will be over." We talked for a few minutes. I sensed the anger she harbored towards Jim. I said, "Debi, you need to forgive your husband. God can't do anything until you deal with the bitterness in your own heart."

Jim and Debi returned to their hotel room. Debi made a feeble effort to ask for forgiveness, but before she could get the words out of her mouth, Jim interrupted her. He said, "No, Debi, I need you to forgive me." He had tears in his eyes as he spoke, and for the first time in years, Debi sensed a sincerity in her estranged husband that moved her deeply.

The Godseys began to talk. They started to cry.

Then they got down on their knees and asked Jesus Christ to heal their marriage and change their lives.

In that moment, the walls came down. "All my life," says Debi, "I had kept my finger in the crack of an emotional dam. I was always afraid to take it out, fearing the flood of emotions I had denied for so many years. But that night the dam broke. It crumbled and I nearly drowned. But God saved me—my life and my marriage!"

When the conference ended the next day, Debi handed me a note that said, simply, "Everything is okay. Thanks for your help."

The Godseys had no idea how much their lives would soon be transformed. They resolved to cancel their divorce. The following week, they drove to Debi's boyfriend's trailer and retrieved her belongings. She moved back in with her husband. Jim and Debi did their marriage projects together; they set aside date nights. Gradually, Jim became the spiritual leader in the home.

Three months later, Debi quit her job as a bartender. On the one-year anniversary of their commitment to Christ, Jim and Debi Godsey brought 40 couples to the FamilyLife Conference in Milwaukee. Many of these people accepted Christ. The Godseys also began a ministry with kids in the inner city called "Kidz in the 'hood" In the first year, they saw more than a hundred children come to Christ.

This one act of obedience—surrendering themselves and their marriage to Christ—has altered their lives in ways the Godseys still don't understand. It all started with a simple act of faith on a cold October night when two desperate people looked to God for help.

A Family Reformation had begun.

1. Will Durant, *The Story of Civilization: The Reformation*, 6 (New York: Simon and Schuster, 1957), p. 452.

2. I want the reader to know that certain elements in Luther's story have been fictionalized. There was no mouse named "Tetzel"; the great man's thoughts during the night of October 30 are conjecture. However, the tale is accurate in key historical elements. And it captures, I believe, the personality, the apprehension, and the courage of Martin Luther.

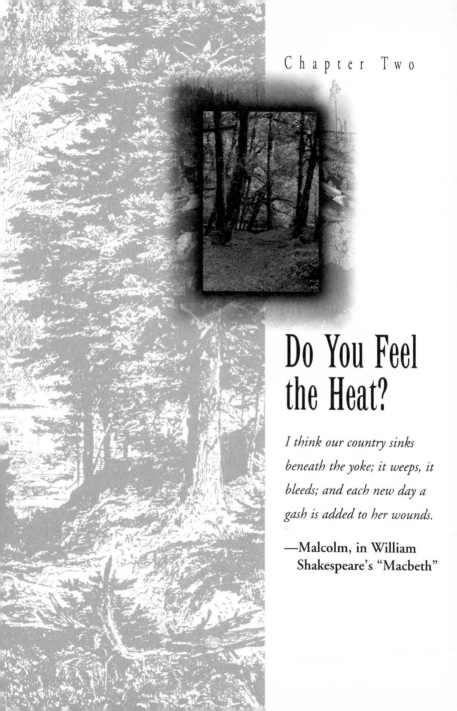

Do You Feel the Heat?

I think our country sinks beneath the yoke; it weeps, it bleeds; and each new day a gash is added to her wounds.

—Malcolm, in William Shakespeare's "Macbeth"

C h a p t e r T w o

*A*renegade monk from the 1500s attempting to redirect his beloved church.

A modern-day couple attempting to break free from the clutches of drugs and despair.

What common threads bring together Martin Luther and Jim and Debi Godsey? Let me suggest three:

First, *all were facing hopeless situations.* From a human perspective each had reason to despair.

In the 16th century, the Catholic church had no rival or equal in power and influence. Who was Martin Luther, anyway? Just a mere man.

And Jim and Debi Godsey had reasons to be hopeless. Dysfunctional homes had dealt them a cruel hand. Surrounded by the counsel of fools, their choices only compounded their miseries.

Who would have given this desperate couple a chance? Flawed and bitter, they were just another couple waiting to become a divorce statistic. Again.

But Luther and the Godseys did not succumb to their hopeless situations.

Second, *this unlikely trio is united by their bedrock courage.* God invaded their souls and gave them a holy grit and gumption. Turning from the lies of their age, each discovered and embraced the truth of God's Word. When life told them to play it safe, to take the path of least resistance, they chose to stand upon the truth.

Finally, *their courageous stand upon God's truth led others to make the same choice and to follow the same God.*

Luther began a reformation that led many people to embrace Christ and return to the Scriptures. Luther's battle cry, "Here I stand, I can do no other, God help me!" inspired a movement of heroic individuals who themselves became reformers and influenced millions.

The Godseys' virtuous stand has not only infused hundreds of inner city kids with hope, it has also influenced numerous couples to embrace the same faith that resurrected their lives and marriages.

Martin Luther and Jim and Debi Godsey are individuals who decided to take God at His Word and refused to go with the flow of the culture. They were just people—like you and me. But they were willing to believe that God could make a difference in their lives and, eventually, in their world.

That's what reformation is all about: individuals looking beyond their circumstances and embracing, courageously, the God of truth, hope, and deliverance. And just as the world was ripe for a Protestant Reformation back in the 16th century, so our culture is ready today for a Family Reformation. We need families who are willing to stand courageously against the forces that seek to incinerate us. Before it's too late.

The Danger of a Blow-Up

To a firefighter, one of the most terrible phrases in the English language is "blow-up." A blow-up is a term used to describe a very uncommon, but lethal, occurrence in forest fires.

While scientists don't fully understand the dynamics of this strange phenomenon, they do know that it occurs when an explosive fuel source combines with two deadly counterparts: fire and oxygen. The combination of these three elements—earth, wind, and fire—can suddenly transform a manageable forest fire into an inferno that rages through the trees at up to 30 miles per hour, faster than a man can run.

We know very little about blow-ups because very few firefighters who have experienced them have lived to tell about it. One rare survivor described a blow-up as "a terrific draft of superheated air of tremendous velocity [that] swept up the hill exploding all inflammable material, causing a wall of flame six hundred feet high.... This wall covered three thousand acres in ten minutes or less."[1]

As you can imagine, a firefighter in the path of a blow-up quickly becomes a sojourner on the way to eternity.

To me, "blow-up" is an appropriate description of what has happened during the last decade at the heart of American society. At some point in our recent past, a combination of lethal elements came together in our culture and created a searing fireball of destruction that seeks to engulf and consume a priceless part of American society: the family.
In the aftermath of this cataclysmic explosion, what used to be a manageable experience—raising a family—has become an ordeal. A matter of life and death.

You feel the heat, don't you?

You feel the heat trying to raise a family in a culture hurling fireballs of sexual promiscuity, teen drugs and suicide, escalating crime, unbridled materialism, abortion on demand, no-fault divorce, gender confusion, increasing parental neglect, and R-rated entertainment that mocks God and celebrates immorality.

You feel the heat when...

- Your child is invited to a slumber party with a friend whose family you don't know, and you wonder about that family's values and you worry about whether your child will be safe.

- You turn on the television and see the nuclear family portrayed as old-fashioned, with fathers and husbands portrayed as inept, sexist, selfish dummies.

- You pick up the local newspaper and read about another young girl who is raped, abducted, molested, or murdered.

- Your son falls for a young lady and you know that the home in which she was raised was far from ideal.

- You pull up at a stop light and look at the driver of the car next to you and wonder, "Does he have a gun?"

- You attend your high school reunion and notice how few of your old classmates are still married to their first spouses.

- You see story after story about homosexual couples and homosexual parents and you find yourself thinking, "These are people who hold respectable positions in our community. And, after all, they do love each other. Maybe they should be allowed to marry."

- You try to decide where to send your child to school and find yourself thinking more about your child's safety than his education.

Like me, you feel the heat, don't you?

As America stands on the threshold of the third millennium, our cultural landscape is littered with charred bones and rotting flesh, the victims of a cultural blow-up. For the past 25 years, I've traveled across this troubled country

encouraging couples to construct godly families. I've interact-
ed with thousands of men, women, and children who are
desperately trying to make sense of their lives. What is fuel-
ing this confusion and chaos? For most, the source of despair
is the family.

Early in 1996, for example, I addressed more than 700
college students at a Campus Crusade for Christ conference
in Dallas, Texas. At the beginning of my message, I asked all
of those who had been affected by divorce—through their
immediate or extended families—to stand. Approximately 80
percent of these young people rose to their feet.

There they stood, the next generation of husbands and
wives and moms and dads, a generation scarred by divorce. It
was eerie. Sadness filled my soul.

After my message, a tall, handsome young man made his
way to the front to speak with me. There was pain and
confusion on this troubled man's face as he told me about his
father's divorce just two weeks before Christmas. His father
had been a leading pastor in an evangelical denomination.

"Dennis, my dad was my hero," he said. "He taught me
everything I know. And now he's gone. I'm the only one left
in my family who is still walking with God." Here was a
young man who should have been optimistic about the
future; instead, his voice quaked with fear as he asked, "What
can I do?" His family had been obliterated.

Other young men and women stood in line that day to
tell their stories of divorce, abuse, desertion, and dysfunction.
They shared openly about their dreams for intimacy in
marriage and their desire for a happy family. There they
stood, the next generation of men and women, wanting
desperately to move beyond their fear, their anger, and their
hopelessness.

Their faces still haunt me. Young men and women are supposed to be full of idealism. Expectantly anticipating the future, they ought to be the next generation of visionaries.

But it is not so. Instead, these young people are paralyzed—seared and scarred by the heat of a cultural blow-up, seemingly unable to escape the flames.

Our culture and even our churches are full of people like this. The heartache is pervasive and immeasurable. Our nation is in trouble. Deep trouble.

Modern Maturity magazine recently surveyed its readers concerning our nation's moral and social decline. More than a thousand people responded. Summing up the results, the editor wrote, "Perhaps the most alarming result of our unscientific survey is that not one person disputed the premise that American society is decaying. What also comes across is a real sense of urgency about the need to get things back on track."[2] One reader added, "We're over the edge and slipping fast into chaos."[3]

Leading Spiritual Indicators

How did we get to where we are today? How did the American family become a triage unit, filled with shattered and disfigured patients?

In 1993, William Bennett, former Secretary of Education for the Reagan Administration, developed what he called "The Index of Leading Cultural Indicators." Bennett's study traced the decline of American society by establishing a statistical relationship between rising rates of crime, teenage pregnancy, abortion, divorce, child abuse, teenage suicide, *and* cultural chaos.

These are some of the fires that have swept through our society. But I believe there are other underlying factors that fan the flames of destruction. Below are five leading *spiritual* indicators; each one is pervasive throughout our culture. Like kindling tossed on a fire, the combination of these spiritual elements has helped create a cultural blow-up—choking, smothering, and incinerating the family.

Spiritual Indicator #1: We Have Lost Our Fear of God.

Proverbs 1:7 tells us, "The fear of the Lord is the beginning of knowledge." This "fear" is an acknowledgement of who God is and who we are. When a believer fears God, he lives in holy reverence and makes Him the center of life. He practices His presence moment by moment. He is aware that the Lord God Almighty sees and hears everything he does, says, or thinks.

But in our culture, we've placed God in a small box and hidden that box in the attic, bringing Him out only for holidays and celebrations, or in a crisis. We are so different from our forefathers. When you read the public documents or personal letters of our founding fathers, you see that God's presence and authority were central in their thinking.

God is not feared today. In fact, He is mocked by our immorality, our treatment of unborn human life, our broken commitments, and the selfish, "me-first" attitude that characterizes so much of what we do.

Even in the Christian community we are strangely silent about the fear of God. There is little teaching on judgment for sin, and the place of eternal torment called hell. We haven't rejected God. But we have conveniently recreated

Him in our image. We have reduced the Almighty to our level.

As a result, this man-made reduction of the Creator has given birth to a superficial view of sin within the church. Why fear judgment if the One who judges is not to be feared? Why be accountable for our actions if the God we serve only sees partially? Why keep our vows, our covenants, our promises, and our commitments if God is too weak to call us to account for our choices?

A.W. Tozer summarized our predicament when he observed that "this low view of God entertained almost universally among Christians is the cause of a hundred lesser evils everywhere among us."[4]

Spiritual Indicator #2: We Have Abandoned Absolute Truth.

When Microsoft introduced its new Windows 95 software in August 1995, it ran a two-page magazine advertisement of two children running with a kite. They had grins on their faces as they ran across a deep-green field with no fences. Emblazoned on those pages were two words that promised what every human being has desired since Adam and Eve: "No Limits."

That advertisement is a vivid snapshot of modern America. It captures the lie of this age: "Be free. Live a life with no fences. Why submit to the old boundaries? You are in charge of your own destiny."

Free indeed! Our "freedom" has created a generation that is enslaved to addictions of all sorts: food, drugs, alcohol, pornography, television, sex, and sports—to name just a few.

Tolerance has become our nation's mantra—our national

virtue. According to this philosophy, everyone is free to decide what is moral and true. Declaring that Christ alone is "the way, the truth, and the life" (John 14:6) is viewed as narrow-minded and intolerant.

And instead of being "salt and light" in the world, Christians bear the imprint of compromise by lowering their standards to match those of the culture. Is it any wonder that individual Christians have such little impact on society? We ignore God's Word. We don't know what we believe. As a result, we hold very few convictions.

Christians without convictions are tasteless and dull.

Immersed in a godless culture, many of us grow indifferent to the dangers around us. Few things really shock us anymore. When actor Hugh Grant was arrested for prostitution, most Americans were astonished—not by the act itself, but because it was committed when he already had a gorgeous, live-in girlfriend. But consider this: Was anyone shocked that Grant was living with his girlfriend? Of course not! Thirty years ago this was revolutionary; today it's no big deal.

Spiritual Indicator #3: We Accept Divorce.

When I was a boy in grade school back in the mid-1950s, only one of my classmates had parents who divorced. Just one. Although my friend's father was successful in business, he lost the respect of the community because he failed to keep his commitment to his wife and children.

The U.S. Census Bureau gives us a chilling historical backdrop to what has become a national epidemic.

In 1900, 1 divorce for every 10 marriages.
In 1920, 1 divorce for every 7 marriages.
In 1940, 1 divorce for every 6 marriages.
In 1960, 1 divorce for every 4 marriages.
In 1972, 1 divorce for every 3 marriages.
In 1976, 1 divorce for every 2 marriages.[5]

Divorce is destroying our churches, our children, and our culture. We have become a culture of divorce. The national media has, thankfully, begun to speak out in various articles about the need for commitment in marriage. But there seems to be an eerie silence—from every corner—concerning the social consequences of divorce. Even the church is hesitant to speak out on this issue.

Why the silence? Perhaps it is because most of us know people who are divorced: they are our friends, our family members, our associates, our brothers and sisters in Christ. We don't wish to "condemn" them.

Our motives are right. But unfortunately, our reluctance to speak out against divorce has unwittingly created a moral climate that not only accepts divorce, but expects it as well. One study revealed that, when a friend gets married, 64 percent of those surveyed expect the marriage to end in divorce. Only 31 percent expect it to last forever.[6]

Harvard historian and sociologist Pitirim Sorokin watched with horror as the divorce rate escalated during his lifetime. He was deeply disturbed by the destruction of the family unit. Sorokin wrote:

An illiterate society can survive, but a thoroughly anti-social society cannot. Until recently, the family was the principle school of socialization for the newborn human animals rendering them fit for social life. At present this vital mission is performed less and less by the family.[7]

That was written in 1948! What would Sorokin say if he were alive today?

Spiritual Indicator #4: We Abandon Our Children.

Statistically, no other parents in the industrialized world spend less time with their children than American fathers and mothers. According to the *Wall Street Journal*, American parents spend, on average, "less than fifteen minutes a week in serious discussion with their children."[8]

This lack of involvement is hastened by rising divorce rates, out-of-wedlock births, and working mothers. But the problem runs deeper than that. Even in many stable homes, parents are neglecting their children by failing to provide the guidance they need.

A recent report from the Carnegie Council on Adolescent Development sounded an alarm about parents who—through ignorance, selfishness, or both—fail to provide guidance for their early adolescent children:

> Barely out of childhood, young people ages 10 to 14 are today experiencing more freedom, autonomy, and choice than ever at a time when they still need special nurturing, protection, and guidance. Without the sustained involvement of parents and other adults in safe-

guarding their welfare, young adolescents are at risk of harming themselves and others.... Many reach adulthood ill-equipped to participate responsibly in our democratic society.[9]

Writer James Lincoln Collier says that America's abandonment of parental responsibility is "unmatched in human history."[10] We can't abandon one generation of children without altering the social, moral, and spiritual landscape of the next generation. But this is precisely what we've been doing now for 30 years.

At a time when the Christian community should be calling parents to renewed involvement, there is silence. It's no wonder the culture invests so little in the next generation, when we in the spiritual community are afraid to speak up and lead out because of private compromise in our own families.

Spiritual Indicator #5: We Feel Powerless to Effect Change.

Of all the spiritual indicators, this one is the most subjective, and the most subtle. But how else to explain our retreat from the battlefield? We feel powerless to effect change. We are guilty of unbelief.

A Christian who is controlled by unbelief will never see God work in and through his life. Unbelief caused a generation of Israelites to perish in the wilderness. The Bible says that "Jesus did not do many miracles [in Nazareth] because of [the people's] unbelief" (Matt. 13:58). Unbelief begins with dangerous assumptions; it concludes that the problem is too big for God, that God doesn't want to act on our behalf, and that we might as well eat, drink, and be merry, for tomorrow we die. Unbelief is the parent of a mundane, business-as-usual Christian life that knows little of the supernatural working of God.

Far too many Christians today feel impotent to make a difference in their own homes, much less in their communities. The battlefront is so vast and the problems are so overwhelming that many have concluded that redeeming our nation is impossible.

We look desperately for some person or institution that will transform society and deliver us from this tight spot. Elect the right president or congressman or local school board member. Appoint the right judges. Encourage Hollywood to produce wholesome entertainment. A few token changes occur, but we can't seem to shake our sense of hopelessness.

Yes, these are indeed dark days in America. Like me, you may be deeply troubled by the fireball of destruction sweeping across our land. And in your quieter moments, you may ask yourself, "Is there really any hope for my family? Can I do anything to escape the blow-up and possibly even save others in the process? Is there a solution?"

I believe there is.

If you are a part of the spiritual majority who has lost hope and courage, take heart and hear me:

YOU CAN MAKE A DIFFERENCE!

But the transformation must start within your own home. In your life. A Family Reformation will occur when you decide to change the way you are living, return to God's Word, and experience Him on a daily basis. If you feel threatened by the fires of today's culture, it is time to start a fire of your own.

Fighting Fire With Fire

On August 5, 1949, a fire was spotted in a remote forest in the Montana wilderness. A crew of 15 young fire-fighters parachuted into the area, ready to tackle what they thought would be a manageable fire.

No one anticipated a blow-up.

Strung-out in a line, the firefighters began their ascent on the south side of Mann Gulch. The blaze was ahead and above them, on the same hillside. Traversing the slope, which was densely covered with Douglas fir and Ponderosa pine, they made their way closer to the fire-line. But the foreman, Wag Dodge, didn't like this angle. And something about the fire made him pause. So Dodge instructed his men to retreat and cross the gulch on the north side.

The terrain changed immediately. The north side of Mann Gulch is markedly different from the south side. Dense stands of timber give way to waist-high fields of "bunch" grass and "cheat" grass. Fire moves slowly through timber; by contrast, it races through open fields. And that's just what it was about to do.

With Dodge leading the way, the crew traversed the north slope, gazing across the gulch at the fire. Then it happened: the inferno jumped the gulch and began pursuing the beleaguered group of smoke jumpers. "Below in the bottom of the gulch was a great roar without visible flames but blown with winds on fire."[11]

A blow-up.

In absolute panic, the men broke for the ridge above them. The 76 degree angle of the slope made escape all but impossible. Howling, spitting, and convulsing behind them, the inferno lapped at their heels; the intense heat tore at their lungs. One by one, the fire captured, then consumed, its victims.

Only three of the fifteen men survived the flames. Miraculously, two of them were able to make it to the top of the ridge. Even more amazing, however, is the way in which Wag Dodge, the foreman, survived the fire.

Unlike the rest of the crew, Dodge realized that escape on foot was almost impossible. So with the inferno bearing down upon him, Wag Dodge did the unthinkable: He bent down on one knee, struck a match, and ignited a fire that, pushed by the wind, burned quickly up the hill. The foreman then stood in a place of refuge—the hot ashes of his own fire —and beckoned his crew to join him.

Unfortunately, no one heeded the foreman's admonition. The two other survivors both testified that "the whole crew would probably have survived if they had understood and followed Dodge's instructions."[12]

A Family Reformation Starts With You

There is a great lesson for us here. Please listen carefully: TO ESCAPE THE FIRE YOU MUST IGNITE A FIRE.

A fire for Christ. You must resolve that flight is impossible, that safety for you and your family lies only in the flames of divine truth. As Jeremiah 23:29 says, "Is not My word like fire?" declares the Lord.

Like Wag Dodge, you and I must kneel in humility and burn a piece of ground. We must bring the fire of biblical truth into our hearts, our homes, our marriages, and our communities. This act of courage nullifies a cultural blow-up by stealing a valuable fuel source; it creates a place of refuge amid the destructive fires of life.

You can't outrun a blow-up. But you can find refuge. And then, amid the life-giving ashes of divine truth, you can stand erect and beckon others to join you. When enough families across our land have set fires for Christ, the cultural landscape will be transformed.

For too long we have waited for the "supertanker" from Washington to fly over and extinguish the inferno. What folly! Since 1965 the federal government has spent $5 trillion dollars on social programs, and things are worse, not better. As Senator Phil Gramm has noted, "If social spending stopped crime, America would be the safest country in the world."[13]

Government is not the answer. If somehow we could make every politician, judge, and leader in Washington, D.C. a Christian, it would not eliminate the need for individual spiritual reformation in your life and mine.

The time for waiting is past. You have only two choices: you can flee for the ridge or you can light a fire. A fire for Christ.

The only true reformers in our day will be men and women with the courage of Martin Luther—dads and moms, singles and single-parents—who are willing to ignite the fire of personal reformation, regardless of the cost. The battle must be fought in the trenches: heart by heart, home by home, community by community.

A great Christian philosopher from the previous generation, G.K. Chesterton, once remarked, "The greatest political storm flutters only a fringe of humanity. But an ordinary man and an ordinary woman and their ordinary children literally alter the destiny of nations."[14]

If you will submit yourself, your marriage, and your children to the Lord Jesus Christ, then you can take the first step toward beginning a Family Reformation!

1. Norman Maclean, *Young Men and Fire* (Chicago, Ill.: University of Chicago Press, 1992), p. 120

2. "Halting the Decline," *Modern Maturity*, Nov.-Dec. 1995, p. 12.

3. IBID, p. 12.

4. Source unknown.

5. These figures derive from three sources: 1) Historical Statistics of U.S. 1789-1945; Supplement to Statistical Abstract of U.S.; copyright 1949; Bureau of the Census; Dept. of Commerce; 2) Historical Statistics of U.S. 1920-1970; Colonial Times to 1970; Part 1, Bureau of the Census; Dept. of Commerce; 3) Historical Statistics of U.S. 1970-1990; Statistical Abstract of the U.S. 1995; Dept. of Commerce; Economics and Statistics Administration; Bureau of the Census.

6. William R. Mattox, Jr., "God Hates Divorce," *World*, Oct. 28, 1995, p. 25.

7. Pitirim Sorokin, cited in a recent issue of *Table Talk* magazine.

8. Cited in *Why Johnny Can't Tell Right from Wrong* by William Kilpatrick (New York: Simon and Schuster, 1992), p. 246.

9. "Great Transitions: Preparing Adolescents for a New Century," The Carnegie Corporation of America, Oct. 1995, p. 9.

10. James Lincoln Collier, *The Rise of Selfishness in America* (New York: Oxford University Press, 1991), p. 252.

11. Norman Maclean, *Young Men and Fire* (Chicago, Ill.: University of Chicago Press, 1992), pp. 73-74.

12. IBID, p. 100.

13. Patrick Fagan, *"The Real Root Cause of Violent Crime,"* an address delivered to Hillsdale College, Feb. 5, 1995.

14. Cited in *The Family Under Siege* by George Grant (Minneapolis, Minn.: Bethany House, 1994), p. 30.

A Call to Family Reformation

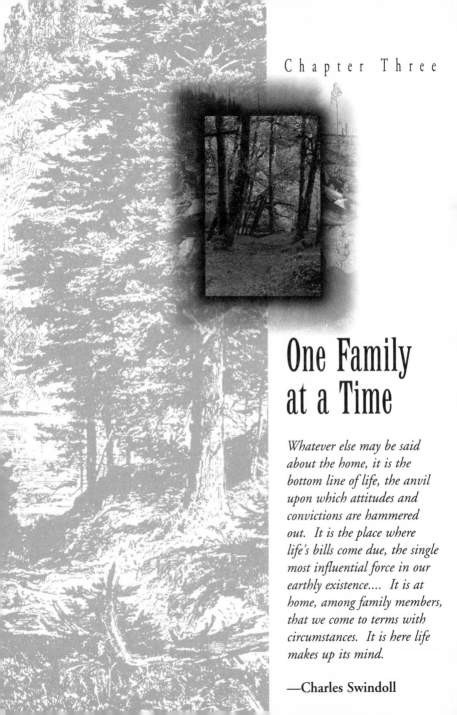

One Family at a Time

Whatever else may be said about the home, it is the bottom line of life, the anvil upon which attitudes and convictions are hammered out. It is the place where life's bills come due, the single most influential force in our earthly existence.... It is at home, among family members, that we come to terms with circumstances. It is here life makes up its mind.

—Charles Swindoll

Chapter Three

*A*few years ago, a friend and I were invited to city hall
in Dallas, Texas, to receive awards for our work in the
area of marriage and family. The building was being remod-
eled, and as we made our way into the lobby it became evident
that we needed directions to find the appropriate room.

We spotted a custodian nearby and asked him for help.
Immediately, I could tell we were in trouble. This man paused
and shook his head. He then pointed across a mass of
construction debris to a hallway on the other side of the lobby.
With a confused look on his face, he added, "But you can't get
there from here."

Later, after we found our room, my friend turned to me
and said, "You know, I almost asked that custodian, 'Well, if
we can't get there from *here*, is there a place we can go so we
can get there from *there?*'"

I smile when I recall this brief episode.

But there is nothing cute or amusing about America's
moral and family dilemma today. We know the problems that
must be resolved and the evils that must be eliminated. We
know what our objective is. But we don't know how to get
there from here.

Since the early 1970s, I've watched our society decay
from the inside out. For a few years I thought, like many of
you, that deliverance was out there: we needed to reform
Hollywood, clean up television, elect politicians with a certain
ideology, and change laws. Now I realize that, although these

things need to be done, there's another step we must take that is far more important.

Today I am convinced, like never before, that reformation must begin—can only begin—with individuals. With *me*. With *you*. John Adams, our second president, made the following observation.

> No matter how heedless, insensate, materialistic, selfish, unjust, and greedy a society may be, if there can be found in it a few clear and powerful voices that speak out unafraid against its corruptions, the spirit and the hope of reform can persist.[1]

When enough Christians kneel on the ground, strike a spiritual match and light a fire for Christ, then, and only then, will real reform begin in America. The flames will lose their carnal fuel; a measure of decency and morality will return to our land.

The real problem is that we are trying to reform society without being reformed ourselves.

The reformation of America needs a focal point, a rallying cry. I believe the focal point is the family. You see, the most pivotal issue before our nation today is not crime; neither is it welfare, health care, education, politics, the economy, the media, or the environment. The most pivotal issue before our nation is the spiritual and moral condition of individual families.

If a spiritual reformation does not occur at the grass-roots level—in individual homes—then the battle for our families and our culture is doomed to failure.

When the Stitches Unravel...

Each family in America is an irreplaceable stitch in the fabric of social order. When one stitch unravels, the fabric is weakened. When many stitches unravel, the fabric tears.

Speaking across the ages, the Chinese philosopher Confucius[2] buttresses this indisputable truth. "The world is at war," argues Confucius, "because its constituent states are improperly governed; these are improperly governed because no amount of legislation can take the place of the natural social order provided by the family."[3]

You can hear the sound of stitches unraveling nearly every day—if you listen hard enough. Most of the sounds are common, but agonizing nonetheless: an anguished wife discovers her husband's adultery; a teenage girl tries to heal her loneliness and gets pregnant; another father leaves home.

Many of the sounds are muffled—rarely do they make the evening news. Others are public proclamations of family heartache.

Two physicians, formerly married, appear in court because the husband refuses to send child support. The judge warns the man that, unless he obeys the court order, he will be sent to jail. "You can send me to jail," the ex-husband replies defiantly, "but I will not pay!"

As the man she once loved is taken into custody, the woman begins to cry. "What have I done?" she asks. "This is the father of my children. What will I tell them at dinner?"[4]

Some construction workers discover a man hanging by his neck in a grove of oak trees. When a police officer arrives on the scene, he sees the figure of an older man, half-running and half-stumbling through the field. With an anguished face the man asks, "Is it Mark? Is it my son? Where is he? Where's my son?" The officer couldn't allow the man to come too close, so the man begins to tell him that Mark had left home the night before and failed to return. He admits they never did get along well over the years, then looks the officer in the eye and says, "I guess we never did have a very good family life."[5]

In Butte, Mont., 11-year-old Jeremy Bullock is standing in line to enter his elementary school. Suddenly a fourth-grade boy walks up with a .22 semi-automatic pistol and fires three times. Two bullets miss. The third strikes Jeremy behind the ear and he is dead before he falls to the ground. Afterwards, the 10-year-old killer sits in the principal's office, stone-faced, showing no remorse. But he does utter three revealing words: "Nobody loves me."[6]

Do you hear the fabric tearing, the voices of despair?
"What have I done?"
"I guess we never did have a very good family life."
"Nobody loves me."
These are the sounds of America's tattered families, first-hand witnesses to the rapid, relentless disintegration of our culture.

What could possibly halt this unraveling? Can we really get there from here?

Returning to the Truth

When you read the Old Testament carefully, you will notice three simple, yet important themes related to the family.

First, it is clear that *God gave us His Word to help us live in a hostile world.* As Psalm 119:105 says, "Thy Word is a lamp to my feet, and a light to my path." His Word is truth. If we are going to experience a Family Reformation, we have to admit we are lost and that we need to return to the truth of God's Word.

The Christian community complains that the Bible can't be read in public schools, but we don't even read it in our own homes! We need God to show us the way—how to get there from here. Timeless directions are found in the pages of holy Scripture.

Second, *God blesses those who honor and obey His Word.* As He told His people in Joshua 1:7:

> ...be careful to do according to all the law which Moses My servant commanded you; do not turn from it to the right or to the left, so that you may have success wherever you go. This book of the law shall not depart from your mouth, but you shall meditate on it day and night, so that you may be careful to do according to all that is written in it; for then you will make your way prosperous, and then you will have success.

The Bible is full of stories that demonstrate the blessings of obeying God's commandments. This pattern has repeated itself throughout history; even in recent decades we've seen that when churches, denominations, and Christian organizations hold true to the Bible and continually point people to repentance and obedience to God, they flourish and make a great impact in the world. But when churches quit teaching the Word, they begin to wither and lose their influence.

The same pattern holds true in families. When a man and woman are married in a holy, lifelong commitment to God, and when they raise a family according to God's principles, they receive His blessing. As Psalm 119:2 says, "How blessed are those who observe His testimonies, who seek Him with all their heart."

Third, *God established the family as His primary institution for passing on the truth of His Word from one generation to the next.* Psalm 78:5-8 declares:

> For He established a testimony in Jacob, and appointed a law in Israel, which He commanded our fathers, that they should teach them to their children, that the generation to come might know, even the children yet to be born, that they may arise and tell them to their children, that they should put their confidence in God, and not forget the works of God, but keep His commandments, and not be like their fathers, a stubborn and rebellious generation, a generation that did not prepare its heart, and whose spirit was not faithful to God.

The implication is clear. When parents stop passing on a godly legacy to their children, a nation suffers.

Many Americans can remember a time when our families and our nation were guided by biblical principles: a time when divorce was frowned upon, when the roles of men and women seemed clearer than they are today, when fathers and mothers placed a higher value on involvement with their children. Even those who did not know Christ as their Savior still believed in a standard of morality based on the Bible.

At some point the family structure began to deteriorate, and an increasing number of children grew up in broken homes. The biblical chain of one generation passing its godly values to the next began to grow weak—and as that chain grew weaker, the culture began to drift from its biblical, moral foundation.

Why? Because as my friend Robert Lewis states, "Family is culture." One family plus one family—multiplied exponentially—creates a culture. The family constitutes the single most important element in any decent and just society.

Societies are destroyed one family at a time; they are rebuilt in the exact same fashion.

You may feel powerless to do anything about crime, welfare, health care, education, politics, the economy, the media, or the environment. But you can do something about your own family.

My friend, the problem is not "out there." The problem is "in here"—in the family. And the family I have in mind is not some political caricature or generic ideal. The family I have in mind is *my* family. And *yours*. The time has come to confront our indifference, our lethargy, our pride, and our disobedience, and to join the ranks of those who eagerly seek a Family Reformation.

Defining Family Reformation

The word reformation refers to the restoration of biblical doctrine; it denotes a "return to a standard." The Protestant Reformation began with a return to a standard, the Word of God. In the same way, a Family Reformation begins when families reshape and reform their marriages and families according to a standard—the truths revealed in the Bible.

A Family Reformation begins when life and truth collide.

Life has a way of editing the truth of Scripture. For example, we know that God's Word teaches that marriage is a covenant. But life begins to edit that truth when a daughter calls home and tells you that her Christian husband is verbally abusing her and the children. If we think only with our hearts, we may become soft on the truth and resort to the world's solution—divorce. "After all," we conclude, "there will then be peace where there is now hostility. Wouldn't that be better for the kids?" So we set aside the truth of Scripture for the expediency of life.

I know this is a difficult situation. I'm not dismissing this problem with a simple theological answer. But I do believe other truths of Scripture must be brought to bear in these circumstances. We must not act according to our hearts; instead, we must carefully weigh the full counsel of God's Word.

A Family Reformation occurs when, at this collision point between life and truth, you courageously choose the truth. Simply stated, a Family Reformation involves *knowing, applying, experiencing, embracing, and proclaiming God's truth about marriage and family.* Each component possesses special significance:

Knowing God's truth means learning the biblical blueprint for marriage and family. The world advances countless ideas about morality, truth, building and maintaining a marriage relationship, and raising children. These ideas—the changing philosophies of man—often collide head-on with the unchanging truth of Scripture. Many of our marriage and family problems in the Christian community can be traced to the biblical illiteracy of Christians.

Applying God's truth requires a concerted effort to integrate God's blueprint into our lives and into our family relationships. We begin to measure our attitudes and actions against the yardstick of God's Word and choose to believe that God's way is best because it is absolute and unchanging. This requires a strong step of faith—believing that God's Word is to be trusted more than our feelings or opinions. It's unfortunate that among those of us who do know the truth of Scripture there is often a shortage of application in our lives.

Experiencing God's truth occurs as we apply His Word continually in our family over time. When God blesses our faith and obedience—in the midst of both trials and triumphs—we begin to see changes in our families. Basing our decisions upon the absolute standard of Scripture results in a number of benefits—peace, harmony, and hope.

The final two stages—embracing and proclaiming the truth—are the inevitable consequences of Family Reformation. Knowing, applying, and experiencing God's Word leads us to *embrace* it as the foundation for our lives. Passionate convictions begin to emerge in the life of a person who habitually makes decisions based upon the truth of God's Word.

As each of us grows in our convictions, the natural result will be *proclamation.* This is where individual Family

Reformation begins to touch the lives of others. God's truth was not designed to increase our head knowledge only, but to transform us so completely that we will seek to share it with others.

Unfortunately, the Christian community has become a "middle of the road" sub-culture. When it comes to marriage and family beliefs and ideals, most of us are strangely absent from public debate and discourse. We don't want to ruffle anyone's feathers. We hold to as few absolutes as possible. Our lives become a gray world with no boundaries. Consequently, we have little influence in the lives of others.

Contrast this with the story of Jim and Debi Godsey in chapter one. When Jim and Debi heard about God's blueprint for marriage, that truth—and the God of truth—began to change their lives. They chose to believe that God offered hope for their marriage, and they applied His Word to their lives by forgiving each other and by asking Christ to heal their relationship.

Over time, they experienced and embraced God's Word as they continued to apply it to the problems they encountered in their marriage and family. And they saw their lives change so much that they reached out to other couples to help them know the God who had saved their family.

The Four Pillars of Family Reformation

Following Martin Luther's "lightning strike" at the castle church door in Wittenberg, the original issue of indulgences quickly took a back seat to the more substantive issue of authority. Luther charged that the popes had usurped the authority of God. By restricting biblical interpretation to the pope alone, and preventing the common man access to the Scriptures, the pontiff was, according to Luther, undermining God's authority.

As the Protestant Reformation grew in strength, the movement centered around four pivotal convictions; these issues constitute the heart and soul of evangelical Protestantism. The four convictions that the reformers fought and (in many cases) died for were: *sola Christi,* Christ alone; *sola Scriptura,* Scripture alone; *sola fide,* faith alone; and *sola gratia,* grace alone. The four "solas" (Latin for "only" or "alone") highlight the matchless preeminence of Christ, Scripture, faith, and grace in God's work of redemption.

Just like the Protestant Reformation, a Family Reformation centers around four pivotal convictions. These solas, or pillars, constitute the heart and soul of God's plan for the family. As you become a part of a Family Reformation by seeking to know, apply, experience, embrace, and proclaim God's truth, these four pillars will become your mandate:

PILLAR #1: Personal Repentance and Purity.

Family Reformation begins in our hearts. It will not begin as a broad-based social movement; it is first and foremost a spiritual movement in an individual's life. It is kindled when dads and moms, and singles and single-parents, get on their knees before God—in abject humility—and cry out, as the prophet Isaiah did centuries ago, "Woe is me, for I am ruined! Because I am a man of unclean lips, and I live among a people of unclean lips" (Isaiah 6:5).

Personal repentance—admitting our pride, selfishness, arrogance, and compromise—is the critical prerequisite for

Family Reformation. God's truth will never be applied, experienced, embraced, and proclaimed by a Christian who is proud—who hangs on selfishly to his rights. If a Christian is to turn to God, he must first repent from his self-sufficency and independence. We must become broken and contrite in heart if we are to truly experience the presence and power of God.

From the ashes of personal repentance, God is able to refashion and recreate a new individual: one who seeks to obey His will, most notably, His will concerning the family. God, in the Person of the Holy Spirit, then takes the repenter and turns him into a reformer—a family reformer.

PILLAR #2: A Return to the Sacred Covenant of Marriage.

Individual Christians must embrace, again, the sacredness of the marriage covenant. Couples used to marry with the expectation that the relationship would last a lifetime. Divorce was not an option. Nowadays, most couples marry with a hope that their marriage will last a lifetime, but, if it doesn't, they figure they can always try again.

The Bible makes it clear that marriage is a sacred vow, a public declaration of covenant between one man and one woman for a lifetime. A Family Reformation begins with a bold return to this timeless truth.

But keeping your marriage covenant is more than just a pledge to remain married. It is also a holy promise to God and your spouse to care for, love, and remain faithful to your partner for life. It means making your marriage all that God intended it to be.

PILLAR #3: Reclaiming the Sanctity of God-ordained Roles.

A critical component of a Family Reformation will be a return to the biblical responsibilities of men and women in the marriage relationship. The Promise Keepers movement has occurred, in part, because men are hungering for a return to biblical manhood. Men are awakening to their failure to lead, love, and serve their wives. There is a stirring within them to return to the truth.

From my perspective, this has been a long time in coming. For the better part of three decades, the feminist movement has undermined the biblical family by blurring the lines between manhood and womanhood. One of the reasons families are suffering today is that because the Christian community has conformed to feminist rhetoric. We have ignored God's blueprint for the responsibilities of husband and wife, father and mother. This subtle philosophical intrusion has left its mark: Most Christian parents are not training their sons and daughters to be godly husbands and fathers, wives and mothers.

A Family Reformation seeks to re-establish the biblical mandate of masculine and feminine roles. Among other things, it unashamedly champions the husband's role as a servant-leader, and the wife's role as a lover-helper.

PILLAR #4: Leaving a Legacy of Spiritual Vitality to the Next Generation.

The Bible says that "children are a gift from the Lord" (Psalm 127:3). As gifts, they must be nurtured, encouraged, and disciplined. According to sociologist Neil Postman, "children are the living messages we send to a time that we will not see."[7] For most of us, our greatest legacy in life will be our children, these living messages now eating at our tables, devouring our resources, and testing our patience.

A Family Reformation recognizes the inherent value of children and seeks to encode them with love, godly values, high ideals, and Christian character. A Family Reformation occurs when you and I return to the truth about children—that they are image-bearers of God, and one of our most valuable resources. They are the conscience, character, and message-bearers of the gospel to the next generation.

Beginning in the next chapter, we will focus on these four ideals, the pillars of a Family Reformation. Only the truth of God's Word can give us the courage to make right choices and hold fast to them, no matter what opposition we may face.

Hold the High Ground

Perhaps you know about Joshua Lawrence Chamberlain, who once served as governor of Maine. Later, Chamberlain became a professor at Bowdoin College in Maine and eventually was elected school president. His final decades were spent shaping the minds of young men and women.

But the most dramatic moment in Chamberlain's life occurred when he was younger. This genial, brilliant man found himself at the center of the most important battle in the most significant conflict in American history. The conflict was the Civil War, and the battle was none other than Gettysburg.

If you saw the movie "Gettysburg," then you know that

a key engagement occurred near the crest of a hill called Little Round Top. On this wooded hillside, Yankees from Maine and Rebels from Alabama slaughtered and maimed one another in one of the bloodiest skirmishes in the war.

Joshua Lawrence Chamberlain commanded the regiment from Maine. Prior to the Confederate attack, a Col. Vincent explained to Chamberlain the importance of defending their position on Little Round Top.

"Sir," said Vincent, "you are the end of the line; you are the extreme left of the Union Army. The line runs from here back to Cemetery Hill. You cannot withdraw under any circumstances. If you go, this line will be flanked; if you flee, the enemy will sweep over the hill and take this entire army from the rear. You must defend this place to the last man."

That's precisely what Chamberlain and his men did. Again and again, Confederate soldiers stormed their position; again and again, the regiment from Maine held the high ground. They didn't retreat and they didn't surrender. The unwavering bravery of these men helped seal the victory for the Union.

I believe we are now embroiled in the most pivotal battle of our generation: the fight for the soul of America. Our "Little Round Top" is the family. And like Gettysburg, this battle demands courage: the courage of husbands and wives who will turn from the seducing voices of culture and make their marriages work; the courage of dads and moms who will reject the poisons of materialism and who will shape the conscience and character of the next generation. We need courage, not merely to hold our ground, but to advance our colors and enlist others in what may be the most important battle we ever fight: the battle for the family.

A Call to Family Reformation

I believe there is hope for families. I believe the Scriptures show us how to get there from here.

In the next four chapters, I'll give you marching orders so you can begin the fight in your own home.

1. Page Smith, *A New Age Now Begins* (New York: McGraw-Hill, 1976), vol. 1, p. 872.

2. Many Christians dismiss the teachings of Confucius for religious reasons. They fail to realize that Confucius was, first and foremost, a social philosopher. His thoughts on the family—as the chief component of social organization—are profound. Historians credit Confucius for the high value placed upon the family in the Far East.

3. Will Durant, *The Story of Civilization: Our Oriental Heritage* 1 (New York: Simon and Schuster, 1935), p. 668.

4. David S. Shrager, *Trial*, March, 1984, p. 6.

5. Personal correspondence from Dave Johnson, a police officer in San Jose, Calif.

6. Richard Price, "Violence Spreading Like Wildfire," *USA Today*, May 9, 1994, p. A1.

7. Neil Postman, *The Disappearance of Childhood* (New York: Delacorte Press, 1982), p. xi.

Needed: A Good House-Cleaning

To reform a world, to reform a nation, no wise man will undertake; and all but foolish men know, that the only solid, though a far slower reformation, is what each begins and perfects on himself.

—**Thomas Carlyle**

Chapter Four

*E*very year during my childhood, when the gray days of winter dissolved into the therapeutic warmth of spring, my mom would re-enact the grueling ritual of spring housecleaning. This was a duty she took very seriously. Blankets were stripped unceremoniously from their beds, taken outdoors, shaken, hung over clotheslines, and beaten mercilessly. Storm windows that had held wintry blasts at bay were de-commissioned for the season and stacked in the basement. Screens were latched in place to allow the refreshing breezes of spring to fill our home.

No dust mite, cobweb, or dust ball was safe from Mom's unrelenting eye. Like a soldier on a vital military assignment, she methodically attacked every corner and closet. From the most covert nook in the ceiling to the darkest cranny behind the couch, her mission proceeded with unbending resolution.

All the while, the fresh Ozark sunshine would bathe our living room with warmth, and a cool, pure breeze would rush through those screen windows, announcing the arrival of a new season. After days of back-bending labor, the task was completed. Our house was clean. I felt it.

Jump ahead with me to the spring of 1994. Early one morning, I stood before a small group of men here at FamilyLife. I had invited them to discuss the concept of "Family Reformation."

Little did I know that a different kind of "housecleaning" was about to begin. In my house.

On the chalkboard behind me, in large letters, someone had written the words "Family Reformation." We talked about those two words and what it would take for a Family Reformation to occur in America. We identified the needs of families. Observations were bantered back and forth like balls at a tennis match. A stream of ideas poured forth. We were hopeful and optimistic.

But an hour into our discussion, the tone of the meeting changed dramatically. Staring at the chalkboard, each of us, one by one, fell silent.

Instead of dreaming about all the things we wanted to occur "out there" in the world, we began to realize that something had to happen "in here" and "in us" first. We sat timidly before a daunting question: "Lord, what needs to change in my life for a Family Reformation to occur in my home?"

As I recall, the meeting ended early. There was very little written on the chalkboard. We had hoped to craft a resounding battle cry for the masses; we ended, instead, with individual introspection, earnest prayers, and somber hearts. What does God expect of me?

I look back upon that inaugural meeting with deep appreciation for the work of the Spirit of God. For, on that day, the real issue became clear to me. I realized that the beginning—the "flashpoint"—for Family Reformation is a return to individual and personal repentance. Family Reformation is an intensely personal matter.

God must work *in* us before he can work *through* us.

Prompted by the Holy Spirit, the Lord began to accomplish a work of repentance in my life, a deeper repentance than I've ever experienced.

Needed: A Good Housecleaning

The familiar challenge of Deuteronomy 6:5-7 became my mandate and invigorated my spirit.

> And you shall love the Lord your God with all your heart and with all your soul and with all your might. And these words, which I am commanding you today, shall be on your heart; and you shall teach them diligently to your sons and shall talk of them when you sit in your house and when you walk by the way and when you lie down and when you rise up.

The phrase "shall be on your heart" means to be "burdened by," or to "carry a heavy load." I've felt this weight in the past, but now I am burdened daily with my responsibility to pray for my wife and children, to read and instruct them in the Scriptures, to protect them from evil. And I'm challenged daily to be the man of God they need me to be.

I was also convicted to practice regularly the spiritual disciplines of prayer and fasting. I'm sad to confess that I'm just a beginner at fasting, one of the most important, yet neglected, aspects of the Christian life. But God has begun using these disciplines to strip away layer after layer of selfishness in my life.

Now, two years later, it has become increasingly clear to me that a return to God alone is our only hope for Family Reformation. The psalmist says it best: "Unless the Lord builds the house, they labor in vain who build it" (Psalm 127:1). There are no solutions to the problems confronting our families apart from a right relationship with Jesus Christ.

Hard Questions

Spiritual housecleaning begins with introspection. Those of us who call ourselves Christians need to ask—and answer—some hard questions.

Why are we nonchalant about the legacy we will leave behind in our children?

Why is the divorce rate inside the church nearly identical to the divorce rate outside the church? And why is there so much silence from the evangelical community on this important issue?

Why do so many Christian men perform aggressively at work and remain disengaged at home?

Why are so many Christian parents negative about having and rearing children?

Why do so many say their secular job is their ministry, but then show so little fruit for their efforts?

Why do Christians talk about family values while their lifestyles are virtually identical to the average non-Christian?

Why do so few Christians possess the confidence that they are on a divine mission?

Why have so many Christians in full-time ministry washed out because of immorality and impurity?

Why is the fifth commandment—to honor our parents —neglected by large numbers of Christians?

Why do less than 10 percent of all Christians regularly tell others about the new life found in Christ?

Does Jesus Christ really change lives? If so, then why do 50 million Americans who claim to be born again have such a marginal impact on society?

Needed: A Good Housecleaning

The prophet Jeremiah asked similar questions about the "church" of his day. As Jeremiah observed, they were a people with "stubborn hearts" (Jer. 3:17) who pursued "emptiness" (Jer. 2:5). Incredibly, as the evils mounted, these people of God "refused to be ashamed" (3:3). "They did not even know how to blush" (6:15). The spiritual leaders ignored the truth of God's Word and ruled on their own authority (5:30-31). And just like the church in our generation, these deceived, distracted believers sat calmly in the house of God, week after week, listening to the teaching of Scripture but ignoring the harder challenges of personal repentance and purity.

In one of the most scathing condemnations in all the Bible, Jeremiah 7:9-10 says:

> Will you steal, murder, and commit adultery, and swear falsely, and offer sacrifices to Baal, and walk after other gods that you have not known, then come and stand before Me in this house, which is called by My name, and say, "We are delivered!"—that you may do all these abominations?

Inevitably, Jeremiah and other Old Testament prophets returned again and again to the one solution—the only solution—to Israel's problems: repentance. Jeremiah 7:3 tells us:

> "Thus says the Lord of hosts, the God of Israel, 'Amend your ways and your deeds, and I will let you dwell in this place.'"

Now, more than ever, the Christian church desperately needs a spiritual housecleaning. This can only come about through repentance.

Turning From Sin

What is repentance? The biblical word for repentance is *metanoia*. It means "a change in mode of thought and feeling."[1] According to John Calvin, repentance is "a true turning of our life to God, a turning that arises from a pure and earnest fear of Him."[2] Correspondingly, repentance involves a turn from sin and a pursuit of righteousness. We agree with God about the wickedness of our behavior and endeavor to live wholly for Him.

The repentant man or woman allows the Spirit of God to scrutinize every relationship, every habit, every goal, and every thought. As J.I. Packer has written: "The repentance that Christ requires of His people consists in a settled refusal to set any limit to the claims which He may make on their lives."[3]

When God's people turn from their sin through repentance, God brings peace and forgiveness where there has been turmoil and shame. Husbands and wives forgive each other and become one. Children regain parents and are raised to fear God and keep His commandments. The estranged are reconciled. The deserted are found. The guilty find relief and freedom. A Family Reformation begins.

All of the great reformations and revivals throughout history began with personal repentance. In his outstanding book, *The Spiritual Awakeners*, Keith J. Hardman says that, as a prelude to revival, "an individual or a small group of

God's people becomes conscious of its sins and backslidden condition, and vows to forsake all that is displeasing to God."[4] History supports Hardman's observation.

For example, when Peter stood and preached on the day of Pentecost, his message was primarily a call to repentance. Acts 2:37-38 says:

> Now when they heard this, they were pierced to the heart, and said to Peter and the rest of the apostles, "Brethren, what shall we do?" And Peter said to them, "Repent, and let each of you be baptized in the name of Jesus Christ for the forgiveness of your sins; and you shall receive the gift of the Holy Spirit."

The first Great Awakening (1740-45), ignited by the preaching of Jonathan Edwards and George Whitefield, created an outpouring of confession and repentance. Edwards had been troubled by much "frequenting of taverns and lewd practices."[5] But the Spirit of God changed many hearts. The preacher later testified to "a glorious alteration in the town"[6] as repentance left its indelible mark.

The second Great Awakening (1790-1840) altered the very structure of American society, spawning anti-slavery movements, prison reform, temperance movements, Scripture distribution, and missionary endeavors.[7] What prompted this dynamic transformation? Listen to the conclusion of Timothy L. Smith.

> If God seemed near in nineteenth-century America, it was not because an elite circle of theologians read Darwin's *Descent of Man.* It was rather due to the

fact that in countless revivals the "tongue of fire" had descended on the disciples, freeing them from the bondage of sin and selfishness, and dedicating them to the task of making over the world.[8]

The transformation began with repentance!

The Beauty of Repentance

In July 1995, Barbara and I traveled to Fort Collins, Colo., for the U.S. Staff Conference of Campus Crusade for Christ. More than 3,000 staff members and volunteers had made the biyearly pilgrimage from campuses, cities, and homes across the country to join forces and celebrate the cause of Christ.

Our first three days together were memorable.

The last few days were unforgettable.

On the fourth day of the conference, Nancy Leigh DeMoss gave a message that ignited a fire. As a staff member with Life Action Ministries, Nancy was no stranger to the need for spiritual awakening. She spoke of our desperate need to turn from pride to humility, our need for spiritual brokenness and confession. Nancy called us to repentance.

Following Nancy's hour-long address, God orchestrated what would become three days of holy introspection. A stream of people asked God, publicly, to forgive them for their sins; they asked fellow staff members to pray for their healing and reconciliation. The gymnasium on the campus of Colorado State University became a temple filled with the presence of God and the sorrow of individuals.

Scheduled meetings were canceled, and speakers who had flown in from across the country returned home without presenting their messages. Men and women repented of their sins: lies, deceit, bitterness, and immoralities were confessed—publicly and privately.

Staff members made phone calls seeking forgiveness for years of bitterness they had harbored against a parent, brother, sister, or friend. Lies and compromises that had been hidden for years were confessed. Brokenhearted parents sought prayer for wayward sons and daughters.

Barbara and I sobbed in anguish as we stood beside a friend who confessed to a life of deceit and adultery. Over a hundred believers streamed from the bleachers to surround this man and his wife and to pray for healing in their marriage and protection for their children.

We will never forget those three days of asking God to "search me, know me, and see if there be any wicked way within me" (Psalm 139:23-24). Oddly, as people confessed sin publicly, there was hardly a person that Barbara and I didn't identify with in some way. There was very little inclination to judge others. Each of us was publicly or privately coming clean and turning back to God.

We left this life-changing meeting with an unforgettable impression of our own depravity, a fresh perspective of God's grace, and a new resolution to obey God. Later, I sought out a friend, face to face, and admitted my bitterness towards him, asking for his forgiveness. Barbara met with our children this past Thanksgiving and tearfully confessed her pride and an attitude of selfishness.

No Facades

That experience strengthened my conviction that changes will not occur in a family or in a culture until people are willing to confess their sins. I remember the Alcoholics Anonymous meeting I attended with a friend a few years ago. I was not prepared for the experience of seeing 300 men and women in that crowded auditorium. The room was bustling with men and women from every conceivable socioeconomic and ethnic background. Their differences were startling. Their unity was riveting.

This group of strugglers had one important thing in common: They were all transparent and brutally honest about their addiction to alcohol. I was stunned by their sincerity. My friend noticed my surprise and said, "Dennis, there are no facades here. We have all admitted that we are alcoholics. We freely acknowledge that we need one another."

There were no masks and no pretenses, just real, broken people, acknowledging their need. That meeting was an issue of life and death for many who attended—and it showed as they hugged each other and spoke words of encouragement.

I have often wondered what it will take for the church to get real, to strip away our pretense of spiritual success and admit that we are sinners. Perhaps God is using the blazing inferno of this base culture to bring us to our knees, to the point where we will ask God to heal us.

Sackcloth and Ashes

You will recall that only three men survived the Mann Gulch fire. Two men sprinted to the ridge; one man, the foreman, ignited a fire. After the blaze burned quickly up the hill, Wag Dodge then laid down in the ashes of his own fire.

In a spiritual sense, repentance is nothing more than climbing into the ashes—our own ashes of pride and selfishness, of greed and immorality, of fear and apathy. Like the raging inferno behind us, repentance is painfully hot; it singes our flesh and exposes our hearts. It burns. It stings.

But unlike the raging inferno, the fire of repentance is life-giving! It sears away our layers of independence and pride, and prepares our hearts to receive the truth.

God is calling you and me into the ashes. The ashes of personal repentance. It's time to quit running. The ridge is too far away. Besides, you can't outrun a blow-up.

God has prepared a place of refuge amid the flame. Throw yourself on the ground. Confess your sin. Experience the cleansing fire of repentance. You won't be consumed. But you will be changed. Forever.

Let me ask you some questions: Is there shame in your life? Do you feel guilty because of some wrong you committed? Is there a corner of your soul that is tainted with remorse, a guilt that you know you must deal with someday?

Has God's Spirit been convicting you of a compromise? *Repent.*

Have you been looking at pornography? *Repent.*

Have you lied? *Repent.* Have you deceived another? *Repent.*

Are you cheating on your spouse? *Repent.*

Are you cheating on your income tax or expense reports? *Repent.*

Has anything or anyone taken God's rightful place as Lord and Master? *Repent.*

Is there someone you've refused to forgive? *Repent.*

Have you spoken harshly to another? *Repent.*

Have you robbed God by not giving as you have received? *Repent.*

But that's not all. Some have not committed a sinful act, they have merely omitted a responsibility or duty.

Have you failed to pray daily with your wife and lead her spiritually? *Repent.*

Have you failed to pray with and for your children? *Repent.*

Have you ignored the reading of the Bible with your spouse and children? *Repent.*

Have you been lazy around the house, failing to help your spouse with household chores and duties? *Repent.*

Have you ignored your wife's needs for relational intimacy? *Repent.*

Have you withheld sexual intimacy from your spouse? *Repent.*

Have you failed to provide for your family? *Repent.*

What is God saying to you? Have you come clean before God? If not, then you can be assured that there will never be a true reformation in your life or your family's life until you confront your sin. The first step toward a Family Reformation is repentance.

The Hard Road of Repentance

During the past two decades I've been involved in counseling a number of people who have been caught in adultery. I have watched men and women lie about it and deny it. I've watched some self-destruct; I've seen others repent. In all of these agonizing experiences, one woman stands out as an example of the power of repentance.

A number of years ago, a woman who had been married nearly 40 years sought me out to confess adulterous relationships that had occurred nearly a decade earlier. Her husband had no idea that she had been unfaithful.

The more we talked about her infidelity, the more I became convinced that in order for her repentance to be complete, she needed to go to her husband and tell him what she had done. Their marriage would never be what God had intended if she kept this breach of trust a secret. She had sinned against God and her husband.

Long before I told her what I felt she needed to do, God had been at work in this woman's heart, stripping away her arrogance and deceit and softening her heart. She agreed that she needed to tell her husband.

Some days later, broken and ashamed, she went to her husband and confessed her adultery. She came clean. She unmasked a lie that had been eating away inside of her for years.

She repented of her sin.

As you can imagine, there was shock and anguish. Feelings of betrayal and anger. And many tears.

But there was also forgiveness, real forgiveness from God and from her husband. A spiritual housecleaning had taken place, and God had broken through in their lives. They aren't playing church anymore. Their relationship with one another is real. God's Word is real. God is real.

To experience a sweeping transformation in our culture, we must come clean in our own homes and in our own lives. Family Reformation begins when God's people cry out, as

David did, "Create in me a clean heart, O God, and renew a steadfast spirit within me.... Restore unto me the joy of Thy salvation" (Psalm 51:10,12a).

Family Reformation begins with repentance.

1. Harold K. Moulton, *The Analytical Greek Lexicon* Revised 1978 ed., (Grand Rapids, Mich.: Zondervan, 1978), p. 266.

2. John Calvin, *Institutes of the Christian Religion 1*, ed. John T. McNeill (Philadelphia, Penn.: Westminster, 1960), p. 597.

3. J.I. Packer, *Evangelism and the Sovereignty of God* (Downer's Grove, Ill.: InterVarsity, 1961), p. 72.

4. Keith J. Hardman, *The Spiritual Awakeners* (Chicago, Ill.: Moody, 1983), p. 21.

5. C.C. Goen, ed. *The Great Awakening, "The Works of Jonathan Edwards"* (New Haven, Conn.: Yale U., 1972), 4:146.

6. IBID, 4:151.

7. Keith J. Hardman, *The Spiritual Awakeners* (Chicago, Ill.: Moody, 1983), pp. 15-16.

8. Timothy L. Smith, cited in *The Spiritual Awakeners* by Keith J. Hardman (Chicago, Ill.: Moody, 1983), p. 16.

For Better, for Worse, Till ? Do Us Part

To call me a judge is something of a misnomer. I am really a sort of public mortician. In the past eleven years I have presided over the final obsequies of twenty-two thousand dead marriages. The trouble is: I have buried a lot of live corpses.

—A Judge on the Court of Common Pleas, Toledo, Ohio

Chapter Five

We have become a culture of divorce. And it is killing America. Consider the evidence:

EXHIBIT A: A father crafts a letter to his teenage son explaining the "rationale" for why he divorced the boy's mother:

Dear Jim,

Before I start this letter to you I must tell you that I love you and none of what happened or is going to happen is in any way your fault. If I had been as good a father as you are a son there would be no need for me to write to you now.

Over the years I have been unfaithful to your mother in thoughts as well as in deeds. Because your mother had complete trust in me I was able to cover up by lying to her. Last May I met a woman in San Jose. Her name is Elizabeth. I am going to leave your mother and go live with her. This does not mean you no longer have a home. Your mother and I still both love you very much. I want you to know that your mother and I will always receive you into our homes with love that is unconditional.

What I have done is morally wrong and I hope you will not follow in my ways. When you meet the right woman, make a life-long commitment to her. I was never able to do this and it has caused much sorrow.

Please do not allow this to change your feelings about your mother and me.

We love you very much and both need your love now more than ever. We will always be your family and will be here for you even though we will be living apart.

I love you,

Dad

EXHIBIT B: The book is titled *How to Dump Your Wife*.

The author, whose pen name is Lee Covington, makes no bones about the purpose of the book. He dedicates it to "all the men who lost it all—their kids, their careers, their reputations, their freedom, even their lives. Because of a wife." *How to Dump Your Wife* is a tutorial for the man whose singular goal in life is freedom from a bad marriage.

Covington imparts practical advice on such topics as dealing with the guilt of divorce, hiding a girlfriend until the divorce is final, and hiding your money from your spouse. Interspersed between flights of convoluted logic ("If we go backwards and force people to stay together, who really gets hurt? That's right, the kids."[1]) and outright denial ("Many kids cope with divorce. Kids have been coping with it for decades. They function. They see their dads; they stick it out and make it all right."[2]), the reader discerns the driving premise behind the book: If you're not happy in your marriage, then leave.

One steady principle applies to most guys who are dying to get out of a marriage: You are not happy.... If you were happy, you wouldn't be dumping your wife. You're just not happy.... This is your happiness we're talking about, for once.[3]

When we ordered our copy of *How to Dump Your Wife*, the salesperson told us that sales were "great." But then, in our "be happy" society, why should we be surprised?

EXHIBIT C: Susan is a sixth-grade elementary teacher in a public school. In class one day, a 12-year-old named Todd wrote a brief essay describing his perspective of his parents' troubled marriage. This is exactly how Todd penned his description:

> "Families are beuatiful.(sic)
> One thing I care about is my family.
> Something you want to hold on to.
> Families are like glass,
> you let go it will brake.(sic)
> My glass slipped
> and I'm trying to catch it."

Todd's family did slip and was shattered by divorce. And then his world began to unravel. When he was 15, Todd took his own life by shooting himself in the head.

Broken promises. Mistrust. Instability. And broken people.

Like a grenade tossed into a crowded room, the twisted, searing, white-hot shrapnel of divorce leaves no one intact. All those in the vicinity of the explosion are maimed. The legacy of divorce permeates every conceivable facet of life, disrupting communities, obstructing education, and dividing families. For many, the explosion is fatal.

At the heart of Family Reformation is a call to restore the sanctity of marriage, keep our vows, and faithfully uphold the marriage covenant.

A Devastating Impact

A bevy of studies confirm the multifaceted legacy of divorce. For example, "children from broken homes... have two to three times more behavioral and psychological problems than do children from intact families."[4] Childhood poverty is five times greater in single-parent families than two-parent families.[5] A study conducted by McMaster University found that "children in intact families were 40 times less likely to be affected by serious physical abuse."[6]

The evidence is final and conclusive: divorce destroys a culture because it destroys families. Harvard sociologist Armand Nicholi III concluded, "Divorce is not a solution, but an exchange of problems."[7]

In a collection of essays entitled *Women on Divorce*, editors Penny Kaganoff and Susan Spano have captured the experiences of women from different corners of our society. With blunt honesty, *Women on Divorce* paints a graphic portrait of the personal trauma of divorce.

Of the breakup of her marriage, Anne Roiphe writes, "I felt as if the skin had been stripped from my body the first months after my divorce."[8] Other writers testify to feelings of intense loneliness, financial distress, emotional confusion, and the loss of personal identity.   Virtually every essay in the collection alludes to the most tragic consequence of divorce: the effect it produces in our children.

Children are the true victims of this social calamity.

Author Gary Sprague recorded the experiences of children in his moving book, *My Parents Got a Divorce.* Their voices echo across the charred landscape, melding into a chorus of shattered lives and forgotten futures.

> It feels like a hurt that won't go away. I felt like my mom was pulling on one arm and my dad was pulling on the other arm.[9] <u>Kelly, age 11</u>

> When my parents got a divorce it hurt bad. I thought I was going to die. I took the blame on myself. That was what made me mad. It was like my family was falling apart.[10] <u>Chris, age 11</u>

> I feel sad that my mom and dad are separated. I don't have two prayers at night; I just have one prayer at night. I feel scared at night.[11] <u>Joseph, age 9</u>

Even the children of intact families are scarred by divorce. Consider the plight of a second-grade boy in an elementary school in Grand Rapids, Mich. When this youngster came home from school one day in tears, his parents asked him what was wrong. Choked with emotion, he cried, "I want two mommies. I want two daddies!"

Puzzled by the boy's response, his parents asked what he meant. He said, "I'm the only child in my class with only one mother and one father, and I want two mommies and two daddies." The concerned parents held their son and explained that it was far better to have *two* parents than *four*.

Incredibly, in the midst of this social catastrophe, very few voices are speaking out against divorce and even less for the sanctity of marriage. Allan Bloom observed this haunting silence in his book, *The Closing of the American Mind.*

> The decomposition of [the marital] bond is surely America's most urgent social problem. But nobody even tries to do anything about it. The tide seems to be irresistible. Among the many items on the agenda of those promoting America's moral regeneration, I never find marriage and divorce.[12]

The Council on Families in America, in a report to the nation on "Marriage in America," adds that "our current national debate has been curiously silent on the subject of marriage. Who, today, is still promoting marriage? Who is even talking about it?"[13]

"Till death do us part," says the Council on Families in America, "has been replaced by 'as long as I am happy.'"[14]

We need a Family Reformation.

Marriage Is a Covenant

Early in our marriage, Barbara and I came face-to-face with a minor problem: our garbage can wore out. Because the defective product came with a lifetime warranty, we confidently returned it to the place of purchase and exchanged it for a new one.

The department store honored our warranty, but, to our surprise, we discovered that the new garbage can didn't come with the same lifetime guarantee. Instead, it was guaranteed for only six years. And, to add insult to injury, the store applied the four years we'd already had the first garbage can to the new six-year guarantee! If your product is flawed, you may need to redefine the terms of your original agreement.

This is precisely what is taking place today in the arena of marriage. The sacred covenant of marriage is being "dumbed-down" and redefined—after the fact—as an agreement or a contract. One company, attempting to cash in on this pervasive problem, has created a unique wedding gift. They call it "Divorce Insurance." Like life insurance, divorce insurance is given to the marrying couple so that, if their marriage doesn't work, they can use this policy to pay for the expenses of their divorce!

Lost in all of the heartache, obscured by the depressing statistics and the subtle attempts at redefinition is the forgotten truth that marriage is a *covenant.* Not a *contract.*

A contract is an agreement between two parties that can be revoked or terminated if either party fails to live up to his or her side of the bargain. By contrast, a covenant is an irrevocable commitment to perform a duty or responsibility, regardless of later changes or developments.

Old Testament scholar George Mendenhall defines a covenant as "a solemn promise made binding by an oath which may be either a verbal formula or a symbolic action."[15] Most weddings employ both aspects of Mendenhall's definition of covenant: a verbal formula (the vows) and a symbolic action (exchange of rings).

The traditional wedding vows used by most couples constitute a covenantal oath, not a two-party contract. The vows I shared with Barbara went something like this:

> I, Dennis, take you, Barbara, to be my lawful wedded wife. I promise and covenant, before God and these witnesses, to be your loving and faithful husband; to stand by you in riches and in poverty, in joy and in sorrow, in sickness and in health, forsaking all others, as long as we both shall live.

When we spoke these words, Barbara and I weren't agreeing to a contract that could be terminated if one of us failed to uphold the agreement. Instead, we were entering into a covenant: a binding obligation to God and one another, sealed by a verbal commitment and a symbolic action.

A marriage covenant is a binding, weighty obligation. Deuteronomy 23:23 says, "You shall be careful to perform what goes out from your lips, just as you have voluntarily vowed to the Lord your God what you have promised." And Jesus Himself said that "every careless word that men shall speak, they shall render account for it in the day of judgment" (Matthew 12:36). God takes the wedding covenant seriously, even when we do not.

Reclaiming the Sanctity of Marriage

The time has come for Christians to reaffirm and reclaim the sanctity of marriage. God says, "I hate divorce"

(Malachi 2:16). The Lord didn't stutter when He spoke these words. It is time for each of us to embrace God's sacred view of marriage, as well as His corresponding hatred for divorce.

Reclaiming the sanctity of marriage in your relationship with your spouse begins with a four-fold commitment.

Commitment #1: Fulfill Your Vows by Staying Married.

If you are married, then you established a covenant. Fulfill it.

Too many marriages begin to unravel when one of the spouses begins entertaining the possibility of divorce. We must reject the notion that divorce is a solution. We must fight tenaciously to restore the ideal of marriage for a lifetime. We need perseverance.

I'm reminded of a statement by Winston Churchill: "The nose of a bulldog is slanted backwards, so that he can continue to breathe without letting go." For a Family Reformation to occur, Christians must not let go. The church needs to return to the model of one man and one woman bound together for a lifetime.

We need more couples like J.L. and Hilda Simpson, a godly Christian couple who recently wrote me a simple yet profound note:

> September 9, 1995, made us 46 years together. I was 15 and J.L. was 17 when we married. We are now 61 and 63. We could have divorced dozens of times but because we love each other deeply, and because God hates divorce, we didn't want to bring the curse of divorce into our family, so we didn't.[16]

You need to keep your covenant. You must keep your covenant. Your legacy depends upon it.

Commitment #2: Fulfill Your Vows by Caring Faithfully for Your Spouse.

Recently, I had the privilege of speaking at a very special dinner party in Miami. The guests of honor were Allen and Ida Morris; the occasion was their 55th wedding anniversary. The Morris children honored their parents' long and blissful marriage by presenting them with a book that chronicled their life together.

The priceless pages were filled with pictures and memorable quotations marking their journey of more than half a century. I leafed through their story and came across one quotation in particular that summarized their feelings for one another. Of his dear wife, Ida, Allen said, "We have been married 55 years and we still tell each other 'I love you' all the time. We say it first thing every morning, and it's the last thing we say to each other before we go to sleep. My only regret is that, since Ida is most likely to outlive me, I won't always be around to take care of her. I know the Lord will do it, but in the meantime, I'm glad he uses me."

Couples who affirm the sanctity of marriage care faithfully for one another. They meet one another's needs for affection, for emotional and sexual intimacy, for protection and affirmation. And they never stop caring—long after the summer has turned to winter, and the vigor of youth is replaced by the predictability of old age.

Vows are more than just a pledge to stay married; they also include an emotional commitment to care for another person. Vows are a pledge to love and to cherish—regardless of the circumstances. They represent the promise of a lifetime of devotion.

I recall a story told about Winston Churchill that illustrates his devotion to his beloved wife, Clemmie. Churchill once attended a formal banquet in London; the dignitaries were asked the question, "If you could not be who you are, who would you like to be?"[17]

Naturally, everyone was curious to know how Churchill would reply. After all, he couldn't say "Julius Caesar" or "Alexander." When the great man's turn finally arrived, Churchill rose and gave his answer. "If I could not be who I am, I would most like to be"—and here he paused to take his wife's hand—"Lady Churchill's second husband!"[18]

I may not have the charm of the Prime Minister, but I frequently let Barbara know that I care about her by telling her, "I'd marry you all over again." I've learned that this kind of affirmation keeps our marriage vows fresh and communicates the depth of my affection for Barbara.

Commitment #3: Fulfill Your Vows by Maintaining Emotional and Moral Fidelity.

For too many people, and too many Christians, adultery is the first step out of a marriage. An emotional or sexual attachment to someone other than your spouse creates intense passions that sabotage trust and marital intimacy. Proverbs 6:27-29 details the consequences of "playing with fire":

> Can a man take fire in his bosom, and his clothes not be burned? Or can a man walk on hot coals, and his

feet not be scorched? So is the one who goes in to his
neighbor's wife; whoever touches her will not
go unpunished.

The irony of adultery is that, tempting as it may be, it
fails to live up to its promises. Peter Blitchington, in his
outstanding work *Sex Roles and the Christian Family*, cites a
study by the Research Guild to substantiate this conclusion.
The guild found that "compared with the 67 percent of men
and 55 percent of women who find marital sex very pleasurable, only 47 percent of the men and 37 percent of the
women with extramarital experience rate its sexual aspect
very pleasurable."[19]

The grass is not greener on the other side of the fence.

Dr. Frank Pittman III has counseled thousands of men
and women who committed adultery. He chronicled their
stories in his book, *Private Lies: Infidelity and the Betrayal of
Intimacy.* Dr. Pittman's conclusion tarnishes the imagined
luster of adultery. "Most affairs," writes the author, "consist
of a little bad sex and hours on the telephone."[20]

The glistening, alluring path of adultery is actually a
barren highway littered with intense loneliness, agonizing
guilt, and shattered lives. Adultery divides loyalties and
multiplies fears.

Will you commit yourself to establishing and maintaining emotional and moral fidelity with your spouse, no matter
how bad your marriage may feel? Two steps are critical.

First, *maintain a healthy sexual relationship*. Learn what
your mate needs in order to remain interested and satisfied in
your sexual relationship. Cultivate the fine—and forgotten
—art of romance. Pursue your spouse with the same creativity and energy that characterized your dating relationship.

Second, *guard your heart in relation to the opposite sex.* According to Jesus, the eyes are the doorway to the heart (Matthew 6:22-23). For this reason, we must restrict our gaze and refuse the temptation to look longingly at other men or women. Don't allow your mind to fantasize about someone else. As Proverbs 4:23 says, "Watch over your heart with all diligence, for from it flow the springs of life." Build boundaries around your heart; make yourself accountable to a friend for your secret thoughts.

Commitment #4: Fulfill Your Vows by Finishing Strong.

In the 1968 Olympics, Tanzanian marathon runner John Stephen Akhwari limped into an empty stadium more than an hour after the last runner had crossed the finish line. When asked why he had continued to run, the gutsy runner replied, "My country did not send me to Mexico City to start the race, they sent me to finish the race."[21]

America has become a culture of great starters and poor finishers. Many like the thrill of initiating new projects but lack the determination to carry them out. Unfortunately, this pattern also occurs in marriage. Americans are quick to walk the aisle; fewer of us are willing to remain committed when times get tough.

We need to be reminded of the words of C.H. Spurgeon, "It was by perserverance that the snail reached the ark."[22]

Commit yourself to finish strong with your vows.

In November 1995, I spoke to nearly 60,000 men at a Promise Keepers rally at Texas Stadium in Arlington, Texas. I exhorted these men to remain committed to their marriages, and concluded my message with a story about Robertson and Muriel McQuilkin.

For 22 years, Dr. McQuilkin served as president of Columbia Bible College and Seminary in Columbia, S.C. All through these years, Robertson's biggest fan and chief supporter was his devoted wife, Muriel. The pair formed a dynamic ministry team: Robertson, the president of the college, and Muriel, the host of a local Christian radio show.

But in 1984, Muriel's health began to deteriorate. A series of tests confirmed the worst: Muriel was a victim of Alzheimer's disease. Over the next few years, she began to lose basic skills. Muriel lost the ability to speak and to reason. She couldn't feed herself. She needed Robertson to dress her in the morning and bathe her at night.

With Muriel's needs becoming more and more urgent and his responsibilities at the college bearing down upon him, Robertson McQuilkin was faced with a formidable decision: Should he place Muriel in an institution? After all, he'd been called to the ministry, and caring for his wife encroached upon his duties at the college. He recalls:

> When the time came, the decision was firm. It took no great calculation. It was a matter of integrity. Had I not promised, 42 years before, "in sickness and in health...till death do us part?"

> This was no grim duty to which I was stoically resigned, however. It was only fair. She had, after all, cared for me for almost four decades with marvelous devotion; now it was my turn. And such a partner she

was! If I took care of her for 40 years, I would never be out of her debt.[23]

In 1990, Dr. Robertson McQuilkin resigned as the president of Columbia Bible College and Seminary so he could care for his beloved wife.

I told the men at Promise Keepers that when I first read McQuilkin's story, I shared it with Barbara over the phone. When I finished there was a long silence on the other end of the line. Weeping, Barbara asked, "Dennis, will you love me like that?" Without hesitation, I responded, "Yes, sweetheart, I will."

The men began to applaud. But I stopped them and said, "Guys, the issue is not what I've committed to do; the real issue is what you are willing to do. Are you willing to commit yourself to love your wife, unconditionally, as long as you both shall live?"

I then asked the married men to stand and recite their wedding vows. I will never forget, as long as I live, the sight of thousands of men, standing and reaffirming their commitment to the sanctity of marriage.

The Courage of a Reformer

Back in the 17th century, Queen Christina of Sweden made an insightful observation about marriage. "More courage is required for marriage," she said, "than for war."[24]

In our generation, Francis Schaeffer came to a similar conclusion. Shortly before his death, Schaeffer said, "The most radical thing a Christian can do in the 1980s is to remain married to his spouse for life."[25] We must fight tenaciously to restore the ideal of the marriage covenant—one man and one woman caring for one another for a lifetime.

Reforming your marriage—in a culture of divorce—may well be the most courageous thing, the most radical thing, you ever do. Don't give up! Don't give in! Don't flee!

You can't escape the flames.

Light a fire for Christ in your marriage. God will honor your faithful obedience to His Word!

1. Lee Covington, *How to Dump Your Wife* (Seattle, Wash.: Fender Publishing Co., 1994), p. 7.

2. IBID, p. 49.

3. IBID, pp. 47-48.

4. "Marriage in America: A Report to the Nation," The Council on Families in America, March, 1995, p. p. 6.

5. IBID, p. 6.

6. "What's Wrong with the United Nations' Definition of 'Family'?" *The Family in America*, The Rockford Institute Center, Aug. 1994, Vol. 8, Num. 8, p. 6.

7. Source unknown.

8. "A Tale of Two Divorces," Anne Roiphe, *Women on Divorce*, eds. Penny Kaganoff and Susan Spano (New York: Harcourt, Brace and Co., 1995), p. 23.

9. Gary Sprague, *My Parents Got a Divorce* (Elgin, Ill.: David C. Cook, 1992), p. 18.

10. IBID, p. 22.

11. IBID, p. 26.

12. Allan Bloom, *The Closing of the American Mind* (New York: Simon and Schuster, 1987), p. 119.

13. "Marriage in America: A Report to the Nation," The Council on Families in America, March, 1995, p. 5.

14. IBID, p. 8.

15. Cited in *Themes in Old Testament Theology* by William Dyrness (Downer's Grove, Ill.: InterVarsity Press, 1977), p. 113.

16. Personal correspondence.

17. James Humes; cited in Richard Exley's *The Making of a Man* (Tulsa, Okla.: Honor Books, 1993), p. 37.

18. IBID, p. 37.

19. W. Peter Blitchington, *Sex Roles and the Christian Family* (Wheaton, Ill.: Tyndale, 1980), p. 165.

20. "Beyond Betrayal: Life After Infidelity," Dr. Frank Pittman III, *Psychology Today*, May/June 1993, p. 36.

21. Bud Greenspan, "100 Years of Great Olympic Moments," *Sports Illustrated,* Feb. 26, 1996, p. 26.

22. Source unknown.

23. A pamphlet produced in conjunction with *Christianity Today.* Robertson McQuilkin, "Living by Vows," p. 7.

24. Will and Ariel Durant, *The Story of Civilization: The Age of Reason Begins* 7 (New York: Simon and Schuster, 1961), p. 504.

25. Source unknown.

A Call to Family Reformation

Role Call

I do not deny that women have been wronged and even tortured; but I doubt if they were ever tortured so much as they are tortured now by the absurd modern attempt to make them domestic empresses and competitive clerks at the same time.

—G.K. Chesterton

Chapter Six

*T*he dark and murky Blackwater River meanders through cypress groves and lonely swamps in northern Florida. During the day, this pristine wilderness can be alluring. But when the sun sets over the Blackwater area, and daylight yields its authority to the blackness of night, an eerie transformation takes place. Moonlit shadows creep across the twisted cypress groves. The strange cries and guttural shrieks of animals penetrate the silence, evoking primal fears and childhood nightmares.

Local residents once feared the Blackwater River at night. And for good reason.

For nearly 20 years, strange things occurred near the river. Over two decades, a number of prized hunting dogs, worth thousands of dollars, vanished without a trace. Their owners, who used the dogs to chase fox and deer, were at a loss to explain the disappearances. Some residents thought the dogs were being stolen; others believed that a swamp creature was the culprit.

In August 1995, when Rufus Godwin's dog, Flojo, disappeared, the strange case was finally solved. Flojo had worn an electronic collar, and when she disappeared, Godwin tracked the collar's signal. He followed the signal deep into the swamp, to a hole near a game trail.

He knew immediately that the culprit was an alligator.

A few days later, the ten-foot, 500 pound alligator was captured and killed. When the gator was cut open, the hunters found Flojo's collar and half of her remains. Incredibly, they also found six other dog collars, one of which belonged to a dog that had been missing since 1981!

Deliberate, crafty, and voracious, this 50-year-old alligator had developed an ingenious technique for killing dogs. "He would come out of his hole," says Godwin, "come up the creek 200 yards and sit on the trail."[1] Blinded by the darkness, unaware of the imminent danger, the dogs ran right into the monster's gaping jaws.

The Gaping Jaws of Feminism

For the past 30 years, men and women have been running blindly into the jaws of something equally dangerous and life-threatening: a deliberate and voracious philosophical "alligator" called feminism. Perched on the path of mainstream American culture, feminism has devoured whole families and imperiled children. Promising freedom, rights, and liberation, it has blurred the lines between male and female, and confused a whole generation of young adults.

W. Peter Blitchington argues that "the most important component of the family is the husband-wife relationship. Any changes in that relationship will produce far-reaching effects upon the community as a whole."[2] Feminism has completely altered the expectations, roles, and responsibilities in vast numbers of American homes—both Christian and secular.

What's wrong with feminism? Why must we as Christians denounce, and even root out, the tenets of feminist ideology in our homes, churches, and communities? A number of answers could be given in response to this question. Here are two.

Role Call

First, *the goal of feminism is a "gender-less" society.*
Writer Susan Moller Okin, in a blunt statement, articulates
the secret passion of these social engineers. Read her words
slowly. They represent the ideal future of a feminist society.

> A just future would be one without gender. In its
> social structures and practices [read "family"], one's sex
> would have no more relevance than one's eye color or
> the length of one's toes. No assumptions would be made
> about "male" and "female" roles; childbearing would be
> so conceptually separated from child rearing and other
> family responsibilities that it would be a cause for
> surprise, and no little concern, if men and women were
> not equally responsible for domestic life or if children
> were to spend much more time with one parent than
> the other.[3]

A quick glance at American life shows the rapid progress
that feminists have made toward their objective. "In nurseries
and schools," writes George Gilder, "in athletics and home
economics, in sex education and social life, the sexes are
thrown together in the continuing effort to create a unisex
society."[4]

Second, *feminism devalues marriage and child-rearing.*
Simone de Beauvoir, one of the philosophical mothers of
feminism, states the matter all-too-plainly:

> I think a woman should be on her guard against
> the trap of motherhood and marriage. Even if she would
> dearly like to have children, she ought to think seriously
> about the conditions under which she would have to

bring them up, because being a mother these days is real slavery.... If a woman still wants a child in spite of everything, it would be better to have one without getting married, because marriage is really the biggest trap of all.[5]

Never before in our nation's history has a woman's role been so centered around economics and the fulfillment of a career—at the expense of the family. Influenced by economic factors, women are having fewer children today. Our national birth rate has dropped to only 1.7 births per couple, the lowest in history.

Driven by this subversive philosophy, millions of American women have sprung from the "trap" of motherhood and marriage into the "liberating" surroundings of the workplace. Career-minded mothers have abandoned children, believing that they could have it all—succeed at work without sacrificing at home. Many other mothers have been forced by their husbands to join the workforce—often at the children's expense—for the sole purpose of maintaining an excessive standard of living. In their absence, children often grow up feeling devalued and unimportant.

I find it fascinating that the group that has so devalued motherhood and children now sponsors an annual "Take Our Daughters to Work Day." The stated purpose of this national day is to build self-esteem in daughters by taking them to the workplace and showing them how they can find value and self-worth.

Strangely absent from the organizer's list of valued occupations for women are those of wife, mother, and homemaker. I would maintain that there are millions of teenage girls today who are struggling with self-image issues because fathers and mothers have given their lives to their careers and not invested in the next generation.

A Subtle Attack

Some may think I'm overstating the case and giving feminism more credit than it deserves. But careful study of the feminist cause proves the point: this philosophy seeks to destroy the nuclear family. We in the Christian community have bought into this subtle ideology and have failed to challenge it with the clear teaching of Scripture.

The family is the chief institution, in God's economy, through which a host of vital objectives are realized. The most important objective is the nurturing and training of children. It is through the family that children best learn the social, moral, and spiritual skills they need to succeed in life.

The family achieves optimum success in nurturing children when a father and mother willingly embrace clearly-defined roles in the home: the father providing sacrificial leadership and protection; the mother nurturing and caring for the family. Feminism overturns this equation by demeaning the man's importance and denying the woman's invaluable, incomparable role. It represents a rebellion against God and His authority over our lives.

Ward and Dalcie Rainey were married for almost 45 years. I was fortunate that my mom and dad were untainted by the tenets of feminism. My mother worked in the home, nurturing two rambunctious boys. She loved and cared for us with the tenderness and the tenacity of Mother Teresa. My father, a private man with a great sense of humor, built his own business and his family as well. Although his father deserted him and his family when he was a boy, my dad provided the moral and spiritual backbone for our family through his model of integrity.

I'm the man I am today because I had a mother and a father who lived out biblical roles in front of me and loved me faithfully and sacrificially. Virtually everything about me—my identity, my character, my personality—was formed through their influence.

Feminism would have attacked my dad for being the head, the leader, of our home. It would have ridiculed my mother by devaluing the time she spent nurturing her sons. To the feminist, fatherhood is irrelevant, and motherhood is anything but a worthy endeavor. It is a trap, a burden to be avoided.

My mom and dad would have vehemently disagreed!

God Made Them Male and Female

Have you ever listened carefully to an evangelical pastor or conference speaker teach on the subject of roles in marriage? Even if his theology is biblical—affirming the husband's role as servant-leader and the wife's role as nurturer and care-giver—he inevitably feels the need to "defend" his position. I've heard speakers say things like:

"No, I'm not being sexist."

"Of course, a number of evangelicals interpret this passage differently."

We apologize. We back pedal. We dilute the truth.

Some even skirt the issue altogether. I read a Christian book recently that was promoted as a "definitive" work on the family. But this author tiptoed his way around the issue of roles in marriage. His ambiguity illustrates a pervasive problem in the church: our fear of confronting this divisive issue.

The subtle ideals of feminism now pervade the culture. George Gilder was correct when he observed that "society can resist epidemics of physical disease, [but] it is defenseless against diseases of the mind."[6]

Now is not the time to avoid the issue of roles in marriage. This is a time to call husbands out of their passivity or dictatorial "headship" and challenge them to lead by laying down their lives for their wives and families. This is a time to call wives back to their biblical responsibilities—to be helpmates to their husbands and nurturing, affirming mothers to their children. As part of a Family Reformation, we need husbands and wives who know what the Bible teaches, who live out their roles without shame, and who pass on biblical truth to the next generation.

The survival and success of the family begins with a biblical understanding of sexual roles. And the centerpiece of our theology is a six-word statement by God in the first chapter of Genesis: " ...male and female He created them" (Genesis 1:27).

Two timeless truths are embedded in this one powerful statement.

First, *male and female are separate and distinct genders.* The sexes are different. Unique. And the differences are much more than merely physical. From birth, boys and girls exhibit distinct characteristics that derive from their unique biological natures. Generally, boys tend to be more aggressive and physical in their behavior; girls tend to prefer more sedate activities, such as playing house or dressing dolls. "At age six, the average boy has about 7 percent more vital energy than the average girl."[7] The difference in energy increases to 35 percent at the onset of puberty.[8] Testosterone, the source of sexual energy, is produced by the male body in amounts ten times greater than it is in the female body.

Many advances in modern science have confirmed the biological differences between male and female. Researchers have discovered subtle differences between the brains of men and women—in both structure and function.[9] Generally, certain skills come easier to one gender than the other. For example, women are better at interpreting the emotions of people in photographs,[10] while men are statistically better at solving mathematical problems.[11]

Also note that God created two genders to reflect His image, not three or four. Unisex, homosexuality, and other sexual perversions are a direct assault on the image of God. A Family Reformation calls men and women to reflect God's image by rejecting distortions of male and female sexuality.

Second, *God created the two sexes with distinct purposes in mind.*

Your gender is not, as feminists contend, a matter of cultural conditioning. The Scriptures make it clear that God created the two sexes with distinct roles in mind. He gave each of us a divinely-imprinted, biologically-mandated set of gifts and abilities that enables us to contribute to the lives of others in invaluable ways. If you are male, then you have been created by God to lead, to provide for, and to protect your family. If you are female, then you have been created by God to nurture your children and to support your husband.

Our greatest joy and our greatest sense of fulfillment in life come when we embrace the roles God has created for us to fulfill. But today there is a revolt against God and these roles. Why? Because these roles require accountability and submission to authority. In a genderless world, devoid of any structural authority in the home, both husbands and wives inevitably fall back upon their own flawed human wisdom.

A Noble Endeavor

When my daughter Rebecca was 11, the two of us were driving home one evening after gymnastic practice. Ever the inquisitive dad, I asked Rebecca what she wanted to be when she grew up. Her response didn't surprise me; I'd heard it a number of times before. "Dad, when I grow up," she said with great determination, "I want to be a gymnastic instructor!"

I pondered this statement for a while. Then I said, "Rebecca, that's a good goal, and if God calls you to be a gymnastic instructor, nothing would make us happier. But I want you to know that if, when you grow up, God calls you to marry a young man and become a mother, then I want you to know that your mom and I would be just as proud of you. Rebecca, you need to make your home your primary focus and commitment."

Sometime later I overheard Rebecca and Barbara discussing the subject of careers. Barbara asked Rebecca what she wanted to be when she grew up. (As you can tell, Barbara and I are *both* inquisitive parents!)

I cocked my head to listen.

"Mom," said Rebecca, "when I grow up, I think I want to be a wife and mother."

The time has come for Christians to reaffirm the institution of biblical roles. To become a husband/father or wife/mother, according to the scriptural mandate, is a noble endeavor.

We must give the next generation a vision of God's structural design for families.

The Biblical Role for Men: Servant-Leader

What is the husband's role in the marriage relationship? When you collate, analyze, and synthesize the biblical record, you arrive at a clear definition. We can state the husband's role in two words: servant-leader. Paul summarizes the man's position in Ephesians 5:25: "Husbands, love your wives, just as Christ loved the church and gave Himself up for her."

Just how did Christ love the church?

Self-denial: Jesus Christ stepped out of eternity into time and laid aside the privileges of deity. He denied Himself, even to the point of death. Servant-leaders deny themselves for the good of their families.

Sacrificial action: Christ gave His life for those whom He loved. Husbands are called—daily—to give up their desires and die to "self."

Servant's heart: Jesus continually set aside His own desires to serve others. In the same way, husbands should surrender their own agendas—and their hobbies—to serve their wives and meet their needs.

I believe one of the major reasons feminism has made such inroads in our culture is that, for too many years, husbands have ignored the biblical imperative of servant-leadership. Even today, many Christian husbands act like dictators in their homes; they are concerned only with meeting their own needs and expect their wives to serve them.

By pointing to Christ's servant leadership, however, Paul gives us a radically new definition of leadership. Review the three characteristics of a servant-leader. What wife doesn't want to be loved like this?

Even after 23 years of marriage, I am still learning the art of servant-leadership. For me, the rub comes on Saturdays. After a wearisome work week, I long for the quiet, unstructured weekend. I love to hitch my boat to my car, drive to my favorite fishing hole, and drown a few worms.

I still recall one Saturday, many years ago, when I did just that. Barbara didn't want me to go; she had just finished a hard week at home with the kids and needed a break. But I went anyway, ignoring her pleas to the contrary.

For the next few hours, my son and I fished on the lake. But I was miserable. After a while, I started the motor and headed back to the dock. Benjamin asked why we were leaving. I said, "Son, your father has made a bad choice; your mom needs me at home."

A servant-leader develops a sensitivity to his wife's emotional, physical, and spiritual needs. He serves his spouse by meeting vital needs within the family. The servant-leader:

NURTURES his wife's spiritual needs by initiating prayer and Bible study.

PROVIDES security by reaffirming his commitment to the marriage relationship.

HELPS with household chores and children's homework.

CREATES an environment of warmth and encouragement within the home.

PROVIDES financially for his family, thus enabling his wife to nurture the children.

TAKES the initiative to resolve conflict and seek forgiveness.

ENDEAVORS to meet his wife's emotional and sexual needs.

As men, God calls us to deny ourselves, live sacrificially, and lead with a servant's heart. To do anything less is to be disobedient to God. To the unrepentant man, these ideals are foolish and burdensome. But to the man who has surrendered himself to Christ, they are weighty responsibilities that lead to life.

At the core of a Family Reformation are husbands and fathers who sacrifice time and energy for their wives and families.

The Biblical Role for Women: Helper-Lover

Three key Scriptures outline the role of wife and mother.

But for Adam there was not found a helper suitable for him. So the Lord God caused a deep sleep to fall upon the man, and he slept; then He took one of his ribs, and closed up the flesh at that place. And the Lord God fashioned into a woman the rib which He had taken from the man, and brought her to the man (Genesis 2:20b-22).

Role Call

> Wives, submit to your husbands, as to the Lord.
> For the husband is head of the wife, as Christ is the
> head of the church, His body, of which He is the Savior.
> Now as the church submits to Christ, so also wives
> should submit to their husbands in everything
> (Ephesians 5:22-24).

> Encourage the young women to love their
> husbands, to love their children, to be sensible, pure,
> workers at home, kind, being subject to their own
> husbands, that the Word of God may not be dishonored
> (Titus 2:3-5).

These Scriptures make it clear that, first of all, *wives are called to be helpers for their husbands.* As women, you need to know just how much your husband needs you. Society considers "helper" a demeaning term; God does not. A wife helps her husband by making the children a priority, by making the home a desirable dwelling place, by taking an interest in her husband's work and encouraging his labor, and by pointing her family towards God.

Second, *wives are called to be submissive to their husbands.* The Greek word for submission is *hupotasso*, which means "to place or arrange under."[12] Submission is not a blind obedience, neither is it a silent suffering. Instead, the word connotes a voluntary subordination to a recognized authority, in this case, the divinely-appointed authority of the husband.

Although the wife is responsible to God for her submission, her husband's assignment is to lead in such a way that makes it reasonable for her to follow.

With few exceptions, my wife Barbara willingly submits to my leadership. She knows that I am eternally grateful for a wife who allows me to lead—and even to fail. Her submission is an enabling vote of confidence in my manhood. And it encourages me to lead.

Third, *wives are called to make mothering a priority.* Mom, your children need you—desperately. They need your time and attention and painstaking devotion. President Theodore Roosevelt said "the mother...is a better citizen than the soldier who fights for his country.... The mother is the one supreme asset of the national life. She is more important, by far, than the successful statesman, or businessman, or artist, or scientist." Make mothering a priority.

Wrestling With the Alligator

We wrestle with sex roles, don't we? The biblical ideals grate on our flesh and prick at our selfishness. Our obstinacy in this one area only illustrates the depth to which feminism has shaped our thoughts.

At times we feel like we're wrestling with alligators.

A few years ago, a 12-year-old boy named Michael was swimming in a small pond near his family's home in Florida. Paddling along with a snorkel and mask, head underwater, Michael didn't know that an 11-foot, 400-pound alligator was bearing down upon him.

The slimy creature lunged for the boy's head. When its jaws snapped shut, the mask and snorkel were torn away. Miraculously, Michael's head came free from the gator's mouth; he began swimming frantically toward shore, with a hungry alligator following in his wake.

The boy's cousin, Jill, standing on the shoreline, began to scream. This alerted Michael's mother. She raced to the bank just as her son reached the shore.

The gator clamped down on the boy's legs; his mother grabbed his hands and began to pull. What followed was a fierce tug of war between a tenacious mother and a ferocious alligator.

Clutching Michael's hands in a death grip, his mom pulled with superhuman strength. Suddenly, inexplicably, the alligator let go and returned to the depths. Michael's mother then dragged him up the bank to safety.

Three months later, the boy was showing a friend the scene of the near fatal attack. By then, almost all of Michael's scars had healed. The wound on his scalp was covered with hair; the scars on his legs and feet had mended. Proudly, Michael showed off three small scars on the back of his right hand. These wounds were inflicted not by the alligator but by his mother's fingernails.

She had literally drawn blood pulling her boy to safety.[13]

Like Michael, children today are caught in the middle of a fierce struggle. Our culture, much like this hungry alligator, seeks to devour them. It demeans the importance of children and, if left unchallenged, will destroy their futures.

Martin Luther said that "the greatest gift of God to man is a pious, kindly, God-fearing, home-loving wife."[14] Joseph de Maistre said that "nothing can replace the education given by a mother."[15] The noblest career a woman can pursue is captured in these two quotations, that of wife and mother. Contrary to the prevailing cultural opinion, God-fearing, home-loving wives, and their counterparts, sacrificial servant-leaders, are society's two greatest needs.

1. "Collar ID Points Out Hungry Thief: Gator With Taste for Hunting Dogs," *Arkansas Democrat-Gazette*, Aug. 29, 1995, Sec. A1.

2. W. Peter Blitchington, *Sex Roles and the Christian Family* (Wheaton, Ill.: Tyndale House, 1984), p. 49.

3. Susan Moller Okin, cited in *Fatherless America* by David Blankenhorn (New York: BasicBooks, 1995), p. 91.

4. George Gilder, *Men and Marriage* (Gretna, La.: Pelican, 1986), p. 115.

5. Alice Schwarzer, *After the Second Sex: Conversations With Simone de Beauvior* (New York: Pantheon, 1984), p. 73.

6. George Gilder, *Men and Marriage* (Gretna, La.: Pelican, 1986), p. 105.

7. W. Peter Blitchtington, *Sex Roles and the Christian Family* (Wheaton, Ill.: Tyndale House, 1984), p. 109.
8. IBID, p. 109.

9. "Sizing Up the Sexes," Christine Gorman, *Time*, Jan. 20, 1992, p. 42.

10. IBID, p. 44.

11. IBID, p. 42.

12. Harold K. Moulton, *The Analytical Greek Lexicon Revised*, 1978 ed. (Grand Rapids, Mich.: Zondervan, 1978), p. 419.

13. For a complete account of this story, see Henry Hurt, "From the Jaws of Death," *The Reader's Digest*, April 1987, p.117.

14. Will Durant, *The Story of Civilization: The Renaissance* 5 (New York: Simon and Schuster, 1953), p. 417.

15. Will and Ariel Durant, *The Story of Civilization: The Age of Napoleon* 11(New York: Simon and Schuster, 1975), p. 332.

Parenting With a Purpose

A child is a person who is going to carry on what you have started.... He will assume control of your cities, states, and nations. He is going to move in and take over your churches, schools, universities, and corporations. ...The fate of humanity is in his hands.

—Abraham Lincoln

Chapter Seven

*I*n the fading twilight, the headlights of an approaching car reminded Jim to reach for the dashboard and turn on his own lights. As the horde of rush-hour cars continued to stream by, Jim reminisced about the teenage daughter he had just picked up from band practice.

He smiled as he thought about all those after-school trips he had made for her over the last few years: dance classes, piano practices, the unending cycle of softball games and tournaments. He glanced at his daughter seated next to him and thought to himself, "She's starting to look like her mom."

Her childhood had passed so quickly.

Usually Jim and his daughter made small talk on their brief ride home. Not tonight. Jim was concerned at the growing emotional distance between the two of them. In one sense, he knew this gap was fairly normal for teenagers and their parents. But he wasn't willing to give up his role as a parent. He knew the conversation he was about to initiate would help close that gap. He had been praying for an opportunity to talk with his daughter without her three brothers around. This was clearly the time.

"Julie, how are you doing with the guys?" he asked.

"Oh, okay," she replied, in her typical teenage fashion. Julie looked out the window as their car passed over a small bridge.

Jim smiled and probed a bit further. "You know, your mom and I have been talking about you and all those boys who call on the phone." He paused, and Julie squirmed uncomfortably in her seat.

Realizing for the first time where this conversation was headed, Julie rolled her eyes.

Her father continued: "Your mom and I just want to make sure you know what you stand for as you get old enough to date. You know what I mean, Pudd'n?"

Pudd'n was Jim's pet name for his daughter. He hoped it might soften her heart.

She smiled faintly.

"I would like to ask you a very personal question and give you the freedom not to answer if you don't want to." He paused again, waiting for her reply.

"Sure, Dad. Why not?" she said flatly.

Jim gripped the steering wheel and glanced quickly into her eyes. "Have you thought through how far you are going to go, physically, with the opposite sex?"

It was an easy "yes" or "no" question for this 15-year-old girl. But it wasn't easy for him to ask. Jim and his wife had talked with her several times about God's standards in the sexual area, but Julie would be dating soon, and she would be making her own moral choices. He wanted to continue exhorting her to make the right ones.

"Uh...well, I guess," she replied. She was feeling even more ill at ease.

They were just about a block from the house, but Jim pressed home the final question. "Well then, would you mind telling me how far you intend to go? Where are you going to draw your boundaries? Your limits?"

He stopped the car a few feet short of the driveway and feigned a look into the mailbox. He knew his wife always got the mail, but he also knew Julie was acting like a basketball team ahead by one point, hoping for the clock to run out. She was stalling.

Jim turned back to her and waited for her response. Even if he had waited for a month, he wouldn't have been ready for her reply.

"No, I don't want to tell you" she said firmly.

It was now decision time for this dad. He deliberated with himself.

What if I press the issue and she gets angry? Do I probe further or double back later?

"Okay," he replied, "I'll take that for an answer... for now."

There was silence in the car as it eased forward and pulled into the driveway.

A High and Holy Calling

How would you feel if you were Jim and one of your children had given you the same response? Would you feel successful, or would you feel like a failure?

Chances are, you might feel like a failure in a situation like this. But you shouldn't. Personally, I would give Jim an A+ for his willingness to address such a critical issue with his daughter. It was a successful conversation because it forced her to think about the choices she needed to make. Jim let her know—in a kind but sober fashion—that he was not going to pull away from her during this pivotal season in her life.

He was going to stay involved.

Godly parents stay involved—especially at those critical times when their children start to pull away.

Jim and his wife have a vision for their daughter, and that vision has fueled their parental involvement since the day she was born. Their desire is to raise a child who will walk in obedience to God in every area of her life, a child who will be strong in character, able to make difficult choices in order to maintain her purity, a child who is able to withstand the destructive pressures of peer influence, a child who will one day raise her own children with the same type of vision.

Jim's encounter with his teenage daughter is a vivid snapshot of what needs to happen in our families if a Family Reformation is to occur. As a parent, it is so easy to get caught up in the demands of daily life—changing diapers, ferrying kids to activities, and resolving sibling disputes, to name a few. In the muck and mire, we lose sight of God's passion and objectives for our children.

From time to time, we need to look above the chaos and regain a vision for parenting—biblical parenting. A good place to start is with God's view of children. To the Lord, raising children is a high and holy calling. They are the legacy we will leave to the next generation.

God's Perspective on Children

God is big on kids. In Psalm 127:3 we are told, "Behold, children are a gift of the Lord; the fruit of the womb is a reward."

Two additional passages underscore God's devotion to children.

And God created man in His own image, in the image of God He created him; male and female He created them. And God blessed them; and God said to them, "Be fruitful and multiply, and fill the earth, and subdue it, and rule over the fish of the sea and over the birds of the sky, and over every living thing that moves on the earth" (Genesis 1:27-28).

"Hear, O Israel! The Lord is our God, the Lord is one! And you shall love the Lord your God with all your heart and with all your soul and with all your might. And these words, which I am commanding you today, shall be on your heart; and you shall teach them diligently to your sons and shall talk of them when you sit in your house and when you walk by the way and when you lie down and when you rise up" (Deuteronomy 6:4-7).

The first passage emphasizes God's desire for parents to "be fruitful and multiply." God places no limits on the number of children a couple should have. He's not concerned about the overpopulation of the world.

It is troublesome to find many in the Christian community who lack God's heart for children. There is nothing in Scripture which indicates that children are optional equipment for a family. Some young couples don't want to have children, and others are "prayerfully concerned" about family size. Often our arguments represent nothing more than selfishness cloaked in spiritual guise.

Now, of course, I'm not referring to those who desire to have children but suffer from infertility. And there may be valid reasons for limiting the number of children in your family. I only want to challenge all of us to evaluate our motives against Scripture—and not listen to the lies of the world.

In the Deuteronomy passage quoted on the previous page, we see the primary reason God wants parents to be fruitful—so they will pass a godly legacy from one generation to the next. The home is the best place for a child to learn about God. To a culture devoid of character and high ethical standards, our best hope for renewal lies in the restoration of godly homes.

Though we hesitate to bring children into a decadent society, the reality is, our kids may well be the ones who will eventually preserve and redeem our culture.

We need to recapture the biblical imperative that views parenting as a sacred calling. Children are worth it! As parents, God has selected us and set us apart for a work that angels can only envy. Think about the duty we've been given: the stewardship of a child's soul. It is a high and holy assignment.

Five Radical Priorities

Family reformers possess God's perspective on parenting. They also pursue five radical priorities guaranteed to accomplish God's purposes and objectives.

Parenting With a Purpose

Priority #1: Radical *Selflessness*.

As with other issues, many American parents are double-minded when it comes to children. We talk about the importance of children; we say we would freely sacrifice our lives for them. But theory and practice are two different issues altogether. In the critical choices we make, we demonstrate that our commitment is not quite as strong as we would have people think.

I mistakenly thought, early on, that God gave Barbara and me six children so that we could help them grow to maturity. But now I believe they were placed in our home to help the two of us grow up! The lessons I continue to learn remind me of the bumper sticker:

MY CHILDREN SAVED ME FROM TOXIC SELF-ABSORPTION

This truth ought to challenge all of us fathers who spend too much time climbing the career ladder or pursuing hobbies, sports, or our own interests—at the expense of our children. It ought to challenge every mother who places her young child in daycare so she can work—not out of necessity, but out of a desire for self-fulfillment or a higher standard of living.

I know a woman who wishes she could stay home with her preschool children. Yet a quick look at her and her husband's lifestyle raises serious questions about their real family values. They live in a new home, drive new cars, and vacation each year in San Francisco. I'm sure there are good reasons for their decisions. But that's my point: Can we justify choices that, in the long run, are not beneficial to our children?

Christians must stop patting one another on the back, affirming one another in our greed, while we abandon the gritty work of shaping our children's conscience and character.

I'm stepping on some toes here; I know there are many women who need to work just to survive. But I also know there are many other mothers who choose to work for lesser reasons—to maintain better lifestyles or to build successful careers. Whether they want to admit it or not, these couples are making a critical statement about their values and priorities.

Am I saying that a mother should not work? No. Barbara and I are in the process of raising six kids. My wife has responsibilities that take her outside the home. But the sum total of all her responsibilities is the equivalent of part-time work. Barbara's chief occupation is at home. When ministry activities, church work, PTA, or travel with me begin to encroach upon her primary calling, we quickly pull out a machete and whack away at these secondary commitments. We are determined not to lose at home.

Priority #2: Radical *Objectives.*

For many years, Barbara and I prepared our oldest daughter, Ashley, for the pressures she would face at college. We had many long discussions with her about the moral choices she would encounter. The fact that Ashley attended a public high school allowed her to confront some of these issues while she was still living at home.

We were confident that Ashley was well-prepared for college, and we were right. Still, Ashley was surprised at the intensity of the immorality she observed on campus.

Students in my generation barely cracked open the door of sexual freedom; today, the door is wide open.

In talking with Ashley about her collegiate experience, a few things troubled me. First, she observed that most students had not been trained to make solid moral choices. Second, when I asked her if the students who grew up in Christian homes were much different than their peers, she made a sobering statement: "There might be a very small difference, but I think with many it's hardly even noticeable." She added, "and I'm not talking about dating...the same holds true in other areas as well—movies, ethics, materialism, and cheating in class."

Why are so many Christian young people indistinguishable from non-believers? I'm convinced that one of the primary reasons is that their parents didn't capture their hearts.

Many parents today are vitally concerned with the education their kids receive and the skills they develop. They spend long hours shuttling them to school and to various extracurricular activities. They look forward to the day when their children will enter the working world and establish successful and lucrative careers.

But one element is often missing in their dreams and plans: character development. Too many parents are more concerned with IQ than with CQ—character quotient.

In the end, your child's character will become the foundation for his or her life. The Greek philosopher Heraclitus was correct when he said, "a man's character is his fate." The leadership crisis we now face in government, in business, and in the church is all related to this issue of character.

As Omar Bradley, the famous World War II general once said, "We have grasped the mystery of the atom and rejected the Sermon on the Mount. The world has achieved brilliance without conscience. Ours is a world of nuclear giants and ethical infants."[1]

Building character into a child means building patterns of behavior that respond properly to authority and to life's circumstances. As 1 Timothy 1:5 tells us, "But the goal of our instruction is love from a pure heart and a good conscience and a sincere faith."

Respect for authority is important because no man is an island. We are all required to submit to authority—in one area or another. And as believers, we are all under the authority of Christ. A child must learn to submit to God in every area of his or her life.

Godly character enables a child to respond properly to life's circumstances. He will display the fruit of the Spirit— love, joy, peace, patience—no matter what he faces.

Character is what will help your child keep within his budget as an adult.

Character is what will lead him to turn to God in a time of hardship and pain.

Character is what will help him pursue his mate and resolve major conflicts in a loving manner.

Character is what will enable him to make that extra phone call or work that extra hour to do the job right.

Character is what will direct him in times of material prosperity and in financial crisis.

And character is what will give him the strength to keep his mind and body pure when everyone in the world and everything within him says, "Just give in to that temptation. It won't hurt you."

Priority #3: Radical *Strategies.*

The Psalmist declares, "My eyes shall be upon the faithful of the land, that they may dwell with me; he who walks in a blameless way is the one who will minister to me" (Psalm 101:6). If there is to be a Family Reformation, then we as parents must seek to model holiness in our own lives. This requires that each of us know God's Word personally and apply it diligently.

Children are like tiny radar units. They lock on. They track. They watch and observe. And they imitate.

Imagine the mixed signals a teenager gets when he answers the phone at home, and his Christian father tells him to tell his boss that he's not home. Or when a preteen has been disciplined for cheating on a test at school, and then watches his dad blaze down the road with a "fuzz-buster." Or when a mom tells her daughter to cultivate her heart and dress modestly, and then the mother spends an inordinate amount of time focusing on her own beauty.

You can't lie and still represent the truth. You cannot cheat and then discipline a cheater. Don't think you can hide your compromise from an omniscient God who passes our sins down to the fourth generation (Exodus 34:6-7). If you want your garden to be fruitful, you can't section off a portion to grow weeds.

Our children need parents who are models. But modeling is more than just doing the right thing. It is also admitting when we are wrong. I try to walk blamelessly in my home, but unfortunately I fail. My son has heard me confess and make an offer of restitution to a neighbor for cutting down a tree that was not on our property. One of my children heard me offer a tearful apology and ask for forgiveness for getting angry and responding inappropriately. All of our children have heard me ask Barbara for forgiveness for hurtful statements I have spoken.

A powerful part of modeling is showing our children true humility, and demonstrating how to handle failure when it occurs.

Albert Einstein said, "Setting an example is not the main means of influencing another...it is the only means."[2]

You are God's model of truth to your children.

Priority #4: Radical *Involvement*.

In 30 B.C., Virgil penned these penetrating words about the formative years of child rearing: "As the twig is bent, so the tree inclines."

Every parent must grapple with our culture over the "bend" in your child's character. Peers are pressing and pushing. We are competing for the privilege of shaping our child's character.

But who will be the primary "shaper" of our children's character? Who will put the "bend" in your child? And which way will your child lean? Spiritually or carnally? Character is cultivated when parents build and maintain healthy relationships with their children. This requires involvement.

A few years ago our family traveled to San Francisco and toured the Golden Gate Bridge. We discovered an interesting fact about this majestic, picturesque structure. Like many other bridges, the Golden Gate is a suspension bridge. Independent sections of the bridge are lashed together by

massive cables and tightly-bound steel wires. This intricate
design creates a secure structure that can withstand powerful
winds and crashing waves.

Wise parents lash themselves to their children with
tightly-bound relationships. And they begin the construction at an early age by holding, hugging, and affirming their
offspring. Reading to your children, getting down on the
floor and playing with them, cheering for them at ball games
and piano recitals, each of these experiences—and a hundred
others—bond children to their parents.

When Ashley, our oldest, was only three, she and I
dressed up one night and went out on the town. I took
Ashley to a smorgasbord, and we gorged ourselves on
chocolate cake and chocolate ice cream. Our next stop was
the theater; we watched "Bambi" and ate popcorn together.

In the car on the way home, I asked Ashley what she
liked best about the evening. I was sure she'd say "the
chocolate ice cream" or "the popcorn." But resting her head
against my shoulder as we sat in the front seat of our
Rambler station wagon, Ashley said, simply, "Just being with
you, Dad, just being with you."

Early on, there is nothing a child desires more than
simply being with Mom and Dad. Wise parents seize this
opportunity and weave strong cables of love and acceptance.
This tranquil period, through age 10, is what Barbara and I
refer to as the "Golden Years."

During these years, the relationship with your child
remains on an emotionally safe level. You may talk some
about the birds and the bees, but the conversations generally
are free of emotional risk to the parent. These are the tender
years of youthful innocence.

But as the tranquil Golden Years fade into the hormonal roller coaster of adolescence, we tend to disengage from our children. We may be there physically—at the ball games, tennis matches, and school plays—but emotionally, we pull away.

This withdrawal is a tactical error. During adolescence, we parents must redouble our efforts, and seek a greater depth of intimacy with our children. When adult issues begin to surface—issues such as sexuality, manhood, womanhood, peer pressure—teenagers need our guidance to navigate the swift currents of life.

Let me illustrate. During high school, one of our teenagers participated in an AIDS awareness and peer counseling training program. We gave him permission to participate because we trusted the sponsoring organization, which has a solid national reputation. But we were shocked when he returned from the day-long seminar and told us about the sexually explicit information that had been presented.

We were pleased that he felt free to tell us about what he had learned. Over the next few days, our relationship with him allowed us to take a potentially harmful situation and build character and convictions into his life. The experience lashed our hearts together and drew us closer to one another.

Troubled by the graphic sexual images displayed during the seminar, I attempted to enlist the help of other parents whose teens were in the group. Since more than 60 of the finest students in the area had attended the seminar, I assumed I would have no problem rallying support. I discovered, however, that not one other parent had called the school or the sponsoring organization to voice an objection. It made me wonder if any of the other children had even told their parents.

I called one parent I knew and asked him if he was aware of the information presented at the seminar. This father was shocked to hear about it; I was even more shocked to discover that he did not even want to talk about the issue with his daughter!

God has given parents an important assignment: we are called to stay involved in the lives of our children. This requires that we initiate discussions with our children about some of life's most challenging subjects—like human sexuality, masturbation, attraction to the opposite sex, modesty, dress, temptations, sexual response, kissing, touching, petting, pornography...the list goes on and on. As parents, we are responsible to take our relationship with our teens to a new level of intimacy—so that we can forge character into their souls.

Priority #5: Radical *Expectations.*

Psalm 127:4 says, "Like arrows in the hand of a warrior, so are the children of one's youth." God designed children to be crafted, aimed, and released for battle—spiritual battle. One of the reasons so many of our Christian youth become spiritual casualties is that they were protected from battle—raised in a bunker and never trained and commissioned to do battle for Christ.

Parents are the strategic architects of the next generation of spiritual warriors. Our children are our legacy.

Many parents set their spiritual sights much too low for their children and families. How many are praying that their kids will become godly men and women, or pastors, or missionaries? We are so focused on worldly success that we lose sight of God's passion—to glorify Christ and to make Him known.

God wants to use our children as strategic weapons in the spiritual battle for the soul of America. Our nation is comprised of millions of individuals who need to hear the gospel of Jesus Christ. Our challenge is to move our families toward the battlefield and labor with them for the fulfillment of the Great Commission (Matthew 28:19-20).

Encourage your children to reach out to their friends with the love of Christ. Train them to walk with God and minister to others. Take them with you on summer mission trips. The possibilities are endless—when we make God and our children a priority.

In addition, we should challenge our children to maintain the same family priorities when they grow up. I recently addressed a small gathering of Christian broadcasters in Muskegon, Mich. Among those in attendance were two young ladies from a leading Christian college who were interested in Christian broadcasting.

As I talked about the demise of the Christian family and the need to return to biblical values, I turned to these two students and addressed them, not as a broadcaster, but as a father. "If God calls you into broadcasting," I said, "then we welcome you and would be honored to serve the King of kings with you. But if He calls you to marriage, then be a helpmate to your husband. Pour your life into him and into your relationship—make your marriage your priority. And if God blesses your union and grants you the unspeakable honor and privilege of becoming a mom, then I want you to know that no position in any worldwide broadcasting ministry could even compare to such a high and holy calling.

There is no higher, more esteemed and valuable call than that of being a mother. Be committed as a wife and mother—to the glory of God."

Raising godly children allows us to link one generation to another. Children are our opportunity to partner with God in the relay of truth.

The impact of a Family Reformation may not be felt in my lifetime, but it may become a reality in the next generation.

Is Someone Waiting for You?

A few years ago I read a moving story written by Don Myers, former director of affairs for Campus Crusade for Christ in Africa. Here's a portion:

It was a fine spring day and perfect timing for a family weekend at the lake. Warm but not yet hot...breezy but not windy. Father is in the boathouse puttering around with various odd jobs. Mother is in the kitchen looking after the baby and making preparations for Saturday lunch. Three-year-old Brother is on the boat dock playing with Sister (five) and Cousin (12).

There is a motorboat rocking gently alongside the dock but a small space of about eight inches has opened between the boat and the dock. Little Brother has always been intrigued by the sleek, shiny boat; he decides this will be a good time to play in the boat by himself (while the grown-ups are busy elsewhere).

A Call to Family Reformation

The attention of his busybody sister and baby-sitter cousin are diverted by their own conversation, so Little Brother decides the time is now. He puts one little foot up on the boat's edge and prepares to jump in...but suddenly the gap widens...his foot slides off the boat...and down he goes into the water between boat and dock!

At the sound of the splash Sister and Cousin look around for Little Brother...but he's vanished. Sister yells for Father, and Cousin jumps into the murky water.

Father comes running but can't see the boy. The cousin says, "He must be under the boat." So Father moves the boat...but the boy is not there.

Father jumps in and looks underwater for his son but can't find him. He comes up for air and submerges again. This time he sees his son...four feet down, holding his breath and clinging to the pier post...waiting on his father.

This is a true story. The father is our oldest son, Bill. The little brother is our grandson, William.

William was unharmed and undisturbed. His father was more than disturbed...he carried William around in his arms and couldn't put him down for at least half an hour.

Parenting With a Purpose

My wife and I wept as we read the letter.

It is the response of little William to his dilemma that I want to emphasize. What did he do when he found himself under water and unable to call for help? He held on and waited for his father![3]

There are millions of boys and girls in America today just like William, who are caught in situations they can't handle. They are drowning—in sexual promiscuity, drug addiction, moral compromise, and emotional confusion—and time is running out. But also like William, they are waiting—for Dad and Mom to get involved.

We must resist the temptation to withdraw. Move into the chaos and confusion. Your children will stall. They'll resist your intrusion. But this is merely a bold front, a bluff.

Our children need our diligent, purposeful involvement if a Family Reformation is going to occur.

1. Source unknown.

2. Source unknown.

3. "Waiting on Father," Don Myers, *Africa Reporting*, Aug., 1988, p. 1.

A Call to Family Reformation

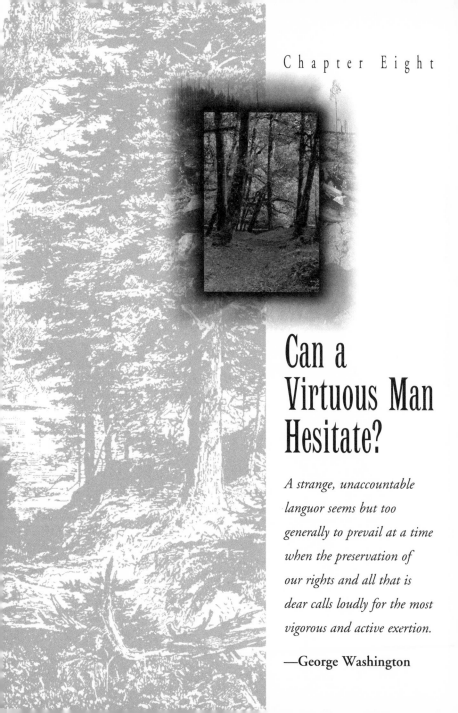

Can a Virtuous Man Hesitate?

A strange, unaccountable languor seems but too generally to prevail at a time when the preservation of our rights and all that is dear calls loudly for the most vigorous and active exertion.

—George Washington

Chapter Eight

With each passing day the situation grew more and more desperate. War seemed imminent. Mother England continued to impose crushing tariffs upon the colonists; the protests of the Americans were greeted with disdain by Parliament. In ever-increasing numbers, British ships, filled with soldiers, were being spotted off the New England coast. Rumors of war circulated wildly; there were skirmishes with the British in Boston and Lexington. Towns and villages throughout the colonies formed militias and stockpiled weapons and ammunition.

The politicians, resigned to the fact that war was inevitable, convened in Philadelphia in June 1775 to chart a course to freedom. The first order of business was clear: find a man to command the American forces.

After debating the issue, the Second Continental Congress extended an invitation to a retired Virginia colonel, a tobacco farmer named George Washington. Washington's response was swift and decisive. Only days before the invitation was tendered, the colonel had written a letter to a friend stating his intentions. In the letter, Washington bemoaned the impending loss of life. Then he added, "But [under these circumstances] can a virtuous man hesitate in his choice?"[1]

Did he? NO! History records the heroic deeds of this man who was willing to sacrifice his life for the cause of freedom.

A Call to Family Reformation

Today, the drumbeat of a different kind of war can be heard across America. In this impending conflict, there are no harbors to be secured and no tree-covered ridges to be protected. No visible enemy will be engaged in mortal combat and no blood will be spilled regaining lost territory.

Nevertheless, the enemy is close at hand.

A war, the war for the family, is waiting to be fought. The battleground is the human heart; the objective is nothing less than the spiritual reformation of the American family. Your family and mine.

But what we lack, at possibly the most critical moment in our nation's history, are volunteers. Soldiers for truth. Washington's assessment of pre-revolutionary America still holds true today. Our first president decried those "who think the cause is not to be advanced otherwise than by fighting."[2]

My friend, if biblical truth truly matters to you, then you must fight! If your family truly matters to you, then you must fight! If the next generation truly matters to you, then you must fight!

Your enlistment to the cause of Christ—and a Family Reformation—is absolutely essential. No elected politician is going to clean up the mess; no reform-minded superintendent is going to transform the public schools; no social system or economic reform is going to solve our problems. The solution for our moral and spiritual crisis begins in your soul and mine.

As I've stressed throughout this book, the single most important reformers in America today are fathers and mothers, men and women committed to personal repentance and purity, the marriage covenant, biblical roles, and parenting.

A century ago, a French poet made a prophetic statement. Looking forward to the bloodiest century in human history, envisioning the breakdown of the family and the destruction of absolute values, Charles Peguy said, "The true revolutionaries of the 20th century will be the fathers [and I would add the mothers] of Christian families."[3] In other words, those with the greatest capacity to bring about change are Christian parents!

Dad, Mom, no one has as much power to effect change as you do. Absolutely no one!

The only hope for your family, the only hope for your community, the only hope for America, is Jesus Christ. His minutemen are husbands and wives, dads and moms singularly committed to the cause. Are you willing to join His army? Are you willing to make sacrifices—individual by individual—for the good of the whole? Are you willing to spearhead a Family Reformation in your home?

The time has come for us to rebuild the wall.

Let Us Rebuild the Wall

Twenty-five hundred years ago, the cupbearer to King Artaxerxes heard distressing news. Travelers from Jerusalem had returned to Persia with information about the Jews in the city of David. The report was disheartening. Two facts in particular troubled Nehemiah deeply. First, he learned that this group of exiles "was in great distress and reproach."[4] They were being victimized by a hellish culture. Second, Nehemiah discovered that "the wall of Jerusalem [was] broken down and its gates [were] burned with fire."[5] The Jews were defenseless against their enemies.

Nehemiah knew that the exiles in Jerusalem needed help. He knew that for the people to survive, the wall had to be rebuilt. The city's defenses had to be restored.

In his book *Profiles in Courage*, John F. Kennedy wrote, "Some [men] showed courage throughout the whole of their lives; others sailed with the wind until the decisive moment when their conscience, and events, propelled them into the center of the storm."[6]

The plight of the Jews propelled Nehemiah into the center of the storm.

From a worldly perspective, Nehemiah's first action was superficial, even insignificant. He prayed. The cupbearer began by fasting and praying.[7] He confessed the sins of the nation, both collective and individual.[8] Nehemiah invoked the promises of God[9], and sought divine favor for the plan he was about to inaugurate.[10]

Then, risking his life by approaching an earthly sovereign, Nehemiah shared his burden with the king. Artaxerxes asked the cupbearer to state his objective. Nehemiah didn't hesitate. "Send me to Judah, to the city of my fathers' tombs, that I may rebuild it."[11] His request was granted.

Nehemiah traveled to the great city and stood before the forlorn inhabitants of Jerusalem. In a loud voice he cried out:

> You see the bad situation we are in, that Jerusalem is desolate and its gates burned by fire. Come, let us rebuild the wall of Jerusalem that we may no longer be a reproach.
>
> The people responded by saying, "Let us arise and build (Nehemiah 2:17-18)."[12]

Two items fascinate me about this story. The first is the determination and courage of Nehemiah. The masses were paralyzed by what they saw: Their wall was in total ruin. Nehemiah looked and saw an opportunity to beseech the Lord God Almighty for deliverance. Others had wishbones; Nehemiah had backbone. The second item that fascinates me is the strategy the inhabitants employed in rebuilding the wall.

To be successful in our construction, we must build with a strategic plan.

Though the Jews were organized into teams and shared the construction of different projects,[13] most of the people rebuilt the wall in front of their own homes. Time and again in Nehemiah 3, the text says the inhabitants "carried out repairs in front of [their own] houses" (Nehemiah 3:10, 23, 28-30).

What an ingenious strategy! Where were the people most motivated to rebuild the wall? In front of their own houses. Where should we be most motivated to rebuild the wall? The answer is obvious: we must rebuild the wall around our home, our neighborhoods, and our communities.

This is where Family Reformation must begin.

The "Bricks" of Family Reformation

To rebuild the wall around our families requires effective construction material. I believe there are seven "bricks" the evangelical community must use to re-establish a spiritual wall of protection.

Because the process of rebuilding is a community project, each part of the community must re-establish the wall in front of their own homes. For this reason, I would like to speak directly to three different audiences: first, Christian couples; second, pastors and lay-leaders; and third, presidents of Bible colleges and seminaries. Each group must build its section of the wall with strategic bricks if the wall is to be restored.

A Challenge to Christian Couples

You constitute the heart and soul of American society. No one has as much power to effect significant, lasting change as you do. No one. You must become Family Reformers. There are three bricks you must set firmly in place for reformation to occur in your home.

Brick One: Rely Upon Prayer.

Nehemiah began his efforts with prayer; a Family Reformation must begin here as well. Psalm 127:1 says, "Unless the Lord builds the house, they labor in vain who build it." Parents must begin by confessing their sins to God. We must repent of our independence and pride, our neglect of the marriage covenant and biblical roles in marriage, and of our charge to parent our children.

List your sins before God and then claim the promise of forgiveness in 1 John 1:9.

Next, make a commitment to pray with your spouse every day. Every day. Barbara and I have been doing this since the day we were married; nothing else has generated more love and affection between us. Nothing.

I believe that if every Christian couple would pray together regularly, our nation would begin to experience a spiritual renewal of historic proportions. As Klaus Bockmuehl notes in his book, *Living By the Gospel*, "It is often true that where there is spiritual exhaustion and defeat, there is the absence or lack of prayer."[14] Nothing invigorates a family quite like prayer.

Begin a Family Reformation in your home by praying with your spouse every day. If you will commit to do this, then sign here:_____

Brick Two: Practice the Regular Reading of Scripture in Your Home.

Adrian Rogers, pastor of Bellevue Baptist Church in Memphis, Tenn., has observed, "Many Christians complain that the Ten Commandments can no longer be posted in their children's public school classroom. But those same parents don't have the Ten Commandments framed and hanging in their own homes."

Is it possible that we've embraced the Bible in theory but not in practice? In Amos 8:11, the prophet refers to a famine in the land: "Not a famine for bread or a thirst for water, but rather for hearing the words of the Lord."

The time has come for Christian families to once again exalt the authority of Scripture. The timeless truths of the Bible must be heard, again, in the family rooms of America. A new generation of children needs to be exposed to the Scriptures.

Read from the Psalms or Proverbs or the gospels at the dinner table, and discuss biblical truth with your family.

Pick up the Book!

If you will commit to begin reading the Bible at least once a week with your wife and family, then sign here:

_____

Brick Three: Uphold the Truths Contained in the *Family Manifesto*.

The *Family Manifesto*, contained in Appendix A, constitutes the heart and soul of the biblical foundation of a Family Reformation. Hammered out with leading theologians, pastors, and church leaders, the manifesto represents a binding statement of beliefs on the family.

Read this document as a family and discuss the timeless statements contained therein. Study the Scriptural references. You may then decide to sign the document, frame it, and nail it, as did Luther, in a public place, such as the foyer in your home.

Commit yourself and your family to the truths contained in the *Family Manifesto*.

A Challenge to Pastors and Lay Leaders

I believe that the churches of America would come alive if pastors and lay leaders began to make families a priority within their congregations. Three more bricks are essential.

Brick Four: Uphold the Sanctity of Marriage.

Over the past 20 years many pulpits have been strangely silent about divorce. This hush has not only dishonored God and the institution of marriage; it has also placed an entire generation of children at risk.

The church cries out for a chorus of courageous voices who will uphold the sanctity of marriage and speak out against divorce. We need pastors who will preach biblical ideals and elders who will counsel struggling couples to seek reconciliation.

For too long we have allowed the culture to define our theology with respect to marriage and divorce. The time has come to return to biblical truth. It is time for pastors to stand together and draw their swords in declaring a spiritual war on divorce.

Brick Five: Establish Church-based Mentors.

Christian couples desperately need other couples— older couples—who will pass on the valuable wisdom they have gained. With so many people growing up in broken or dysfunctional homes, many adults have little knowledge of how to build strong marriages, how to fulfill their roles as husbands and wives, or how to raise godly children. There is a critical need for a volunteer corps of Green Berets— marriage and family mentors—who can do battle for families and provide encouragement at critical stress points.

I'd love to see churches begin mentoring programs for a variety of different groups:

Engaged couples
Newly-married couples
New parents
Parents of pre-adolescents
Parents of teenagers

Men

Women

Couples seeking reconciliation

While working on this very section of the book, we heard from a pastor of a large church in Montgomery, Ala., who is serious about the mentoring concept. He has trained dozens of couples to lead small groups of engaged couples through an eight-week course that teaches them the biblical model of marriage and helps them decide whether they should marry.

The pastor estimated that his church will take 120 engaged couples through this course in 1996; he also mentioned that several other churches in the area are interested in starting the same program.

Mentoring is one of our most urgent needs in the church. It may well be the most important strategy the church can implement to retrain and heal a generation wounded by divorce, dysfunctional families, and a hostile culture.

Brick Six: Establish a Coalition of Churches for the Family.

Pastors and lay leaders could give impetus to a Family Reformation by establishing local coalitions for the family. Neighborhood and community churches could band together and publicly affirm their commitment to the family.

One such declaration occurred in a ceremony at the Oklahoma state capital on October 14, 1994. Fifty-six people affixed their names to the *Family Manifesto* and then read the document publicly.

In several communities, including Montgomery, Ala., and Modesto, Calif., churches have formed coalitions and set common standards for premarital preparation.

Churches in a coalition could also set aside one Sunday a year to pray for Family Reformation. This "Family Reformation Sunday" could become an annual event, bringing Christians together who are committed to spiritual renewal, cleansing, and the restoration of the family. Congregations must be led to their knees to pray for the family.

A Challenge to Presidents of Bible Colleges and Seminaries

The work of Family Reformation is a work of individuals and families. But for the reformation to succeed, undergraduate and graduate Christian schools and seminaries must also recognize the need to be involved in this effort. One brick is essential.

Brick Seven: Emphasize Family at Educational and Training Institutions.

Two important steps are essential. First, *young people must be trained in the basics of the Christian family.* Divorce has shattered the biblical ideals of too many young people today. An entire generation of students lacks a model for marriage and family.

What is needed is a series of biblical courses that deal with relationships, conflict resolution, the fundamentals of marriage, masculine and feminine identity, biblical roles in marriage, and Christian parenting. These young people must be implored to know, apply, experience, embrace, and proclaim God's truth before they have made marital commitments and become parents.

Second, *we must establish a theology of the family and require all seminarians to formulate their beliefs and convictions about the family before graduation.*

Seminaries need to make a "generational" commitment to the rebuilding of the family. A good starting point would be the development of the biblical doctrine of marriage and family. Our schools teach ecclesiology (the doctrine of the church), soteriology (the doctrine of salvation), hamartiology (the doctrine of sin), and eschatology (the doctrine of the Second Coming). But there is no "doctrine of the family."

If the Christian community continues to refuse to define critical issues concerning the family, then our culture will continue to do it for us. Leaders of seminaries need to help families restore the wall by taking a stand for truth in this critical area.

Standing for the Truth

Throughout the pages of this book, I have challenged individual Christians to join a Family Reformation. I believe that if you will ignite a fire for Christ—in your heart, your home, and your community—then God will restore our families. The rolling fireball of destruction that seeks to engulf us will lose its power; our communities and our nation will experience the moral, spiritual, and social rejuvenation that is so urgently needed.

But change can only occur heart by heart, individual by individual, home by home.

Listen to the blunt conclusion of James Lincoln Collier in his fine book, *The Rise of Selfishness in America.*

> A damaged society cannot be improved by tinkering with monetary policy or in somehow "changing the system." It is critically important for us to understand that there is no such thing as a "system."...A society can only be improved when those who constitute it decide to improve it. And this means making sacrifices individual by individual for the good of the whole. A government cannot legislate against the indulgent self. Only the people, acting from the springs of their own hearts, can do that. Will they? That is a question I cannot answer.[15]

Family Reformation must begin with individual sacrifice. But sacrifice takes courage. Your courage. The easiest thing to do is nothing.

It takes courage to confess and repent of sin.

It takes courage to keep your wedding vows and uphold your biblical roles in the family.

It takes courage to raise godly children in the midst of an infernal, godless culture.

It takes courage to stand for the truth when every voice around you screams, "COMPROMISE! SURRENDER! TAKE THE EASY WAY OUT!"

In the early 1970s, the Iraqi government arrested a group of American students on trumped-up espionage charges. The wicked regime of Saddam Hussein wanted confessions, and to elicit the desired admissions of guilt, the students were tortured.

The prisoners were told that if they confessed, they could go free. Compromise the truth. Admit to a falsehood.

The promise of freedom became irresistible.

One by one, as the pressures and the pain mounted, every prisoner confessed to crimes he didn't commit. Every prisoner except one.

For this one man, the torture intensified. The loneliness of isolation became unbearable. He came close to breaking.

Recounting his friend's story in *The Wall Street Journal*, Mark Helprin writes, "Then they announced that they were finished with his case, that he could simply confess or die. A confession lay before him as they raised a pistol to his head, cocked the hammer, and started a countdown. He had heard executions from his cell. 'Sign your name,' he was told, 'and you will live.' But he refused. He closed his eyes, grimaced, and prepared to die. They pulled the trigger. When he heard the click he thought he was dead. The gun, however, had not been loaded."[16]

Helprin's friend was eventually released. He discovered afterwards that every other prisoner who had confessed was hanged in the public square.

Only he survived.

The moral of the story is clear: compromise represents a far greater risk than courage does. As difficult as it is to stand for truth, it is much harder to live or die with the consequences of moral failure.

Nearly 500 years ago, a wayward church held a "gun" to the head of a simple Augustinian monk. Faced with the choice between surrender or excommunication, Martin Luther spoke the words that changed the course of history. "My conscience is captive to the Word of God," he said. "I cannot and will not recant anything, for to go against conscience is neither right nor safe. Here I stand. I can do no other. God help me."

My friend, when every voice around you screams, "COMPROMISE! SURRENDER! TAKE THE EASY WAY OUT!", when marriage is hard and parenting is harder, when your wedding vows could easily be broken, STAND FOR THE TRUTH!

God will reward your faithfulness.

Your spouse and your children will thank you.

A precious part of America's soul will be restored.

And one more spark will kindle the flame of a Family Reformation!

1. Charles Cecil Wall, *George Washington: Citizen-Soldier* (Charlottesville, N.C.: University Press of Virginia, 1980), p. 39.

2. Douglas Southall Freeman, *George Washington: A Biography* (New York: Charles Scribner's Sons; 1951), vol. 4, p. 435.

3. Cited in *Idols for Destruction* by Herbert Schlossberg (Washington, D.C.: Regnery Gateway, 1990), p. 333.

4. Nehemiah 1:3

5. IBID.

6. John F. Kennedy, *Profiles in Courage* (New York: Harper and Row, 1961), pp. 20-21.

7. Nehemiah 1:4

8. Nehemiah 1:6

9. Nehemiah 1:8-9

10. Nehemiah 1:10

11. Nehemiah 2:5

12. Nehemiah 2:18

13. Nehemiah 3:1,3,6,8

14. Klaus Bockmuehl, *Living by the Gospel* (Colorado Springs, Colo.: Helmers and Howard, 1986), p. 62.

15. James Lincoln Collier, *The Rise of Selfishness in America* (New York: Oxford, 1991), p. 264.

16. Mark Helprin, "To the New Congressional Majority," *The Wall Street Journal,* Jan. 3, 1995, p. 7.

The *Family Manifesto*

We have plunged into a danger zone in which increasing numbers of people—whether they are part of the body of believers or not—are incapable of disentangling cultural mores from fundamental Christian values.

—**George Barna**

A p p e n d i x

*I*n 1933 a handful of intellectuals, educators, and philosophers joined ranks to craft a document they called the *Humanist Manifesto.* Present at this historic meeting were a small, but influential, group of social engineers, men like John Dewey, the father of American progressive education, B.F. Skinner, the father of behavioral psychology, and Sir Julian Huxley, the world-renown biologist.

Though drawn from a wide array of disciplines, the authors of that manifesto shared a number of philosophical beliefs. First, they were ardent anti-theists—men and women who disavowed the God of the Bible and the authority of Scripture. Second, they believed, in the words of the ancient philosopher Protagoras, that "man is the measure of all things," the final authority in heaven and on earth. Third, this group shared the conviction that reason alone can provide the solutions to mankind's most urgent problems.

Though few Americans are familiar with the *Humanist Manifesto,* the ideals contained therein have had a profound impact upon American society. By deifying man and humanizing God, the authors fostered the rampant self-indulgence, self-centeredness, and greed that now infects our culture.

This narcissistic plague has had its greatest—and most negative—effect upon the family.

The authors infused their beliefs into the manifesto and signed their names to the document. This bold act galvanized the courage and unified the beliefs of a relatively small number of people, a group of people whose ideas ultimately changed the world.

Courage—of any kind—begins with a clear definition of personal belief.

A Different Kind of Manifesto

Sixty years later, on February 2, 1993, a different group of people came together to sign a different kind of manifesto. The meeting occurred in Little Rock, Ark. The participants were the staff of FamilyLife. For more than a year, members of our ministry worked diligently with me to craft what we call the *Family Manifesto*. This document, which bears the imprint of church historians, theologians, professors, pastors, and laymen, represents a biblical statement on marriage and family.

The final draft was reproduced on parchment, framed, and nailed to the wall in the foyer of our building.

At the commemorative signing, each section of the manifesto was read publicly. Dr. Bill Bright, founder and president of Campus Crusade for Christ, and his wife, Vonette, were the first to affix their names to the document. Throughout the occasion, we paused and prayed that God would help us realize these ideals in our own families. One by one, individuals and couples came forward to sign the manifesto.

It was an emotional experience. While on our knees that evening, Dr. Bright leaned over to me and said, "Dennis, I believe this is a historic event. I predict this will change the course of millions of families around the world!"

Since that evening we have organized a number of public signings of the *Family Manifesto*. Across our country and around the world, men and women from every walk of life—mothers and fathers, engineers and salesmen, truck-drivers and factory workers, professors and doctors, pastors and politicians—have signed their names to this document and said, in effect, "I believe and I am committed to these ideals." The original document now contains more than 800 signatures and represents more than 25 countries.

The *Family Manifesto* is reproduced below. I encourage you to familiarize yourself with this document. Read it to yourself. Read it to your family. You may even want to frame it and nail it in a prominent location in your home.

As Dr. Bright stated, the *Family Manifesto* may well make a difference in the lives of millions of Americans. This is my hope and prayer. But I also know that such sweeping reformation must begin with a single spark.

Do you have the courage to embrace the truth and ignite a fire of reformation?

Family Manifesto

Preface

During the latter half of the twentieth century, American culture has suffered an unrelenting decline. Although scientific and technological advances have created an outer veneer of prosperity and progress, our inner moral values and convictions have rapidly crumbled. Once, most Americans based their sense of right and wrong on Judeo-Christian principles, which provided them with a solid, biblical foundation for life. Today, a growing number of Americans see morality and ethics as relative and subjective, and have developed their own version of "morality" with little regard to absolute standards.

This idea of moral tolerance has been eroding the foundation of the American family and society. Many Americans today have little or no concept of how to maintain a successful marriage, or how to raise children to become responsible adults. In addition, a growing number of educators, politicians, and members of the media are attacking and redefining the family, creating a vast amount of confusion about what a family is. Many people today proclaim that "family values" are important, but the gradual shift to moral relativism has led to a great debate about what "family values" ought to be.

Abraham Lincoln once said, "The strength of a nation lies in the homes of its people." It is our conviction that the family is the backbone of the Christian church and of society as a whole. History shows that, for any society to survive, it must uphold, strengthen, and continue to build upon the biblical institutions of marriage and family.

The Bible begins in Genesis with the marriage of a man and a woman and ends in the book of Revelation with the marriage of Christ and His bride, the Church. In between, God has given us a set of timeless blueprints for family life which, if followed in a spirit of humility and obedience, provide us with the only true way to maintain healthy family relationships.

The following document affirms this biblical model and challenges us to consider how we should live within the walls of our own homes. It is offered in a spirit of love and humility, not of judgment or contention. Furthermore, it is not intended to be a comprehensive doctrinal statement about what the Bible says about marriage, family, and related subjects.

Unquestionably, this document attempts to face critical cultural issues. We invite response from anyone who wishes to affirm the truths of marriage and family from the Scriptures. It is our hope that this document will serve to accurately represent the truth God has revealed to us in Scripture, will provide insight into what a biblical family looks like, and will show how we can honor and glorify Him in our family relationships.

We freely acknowledge that we, like all people, have often denied the biblical truths of family life by the way we live. We desire, however, to live by God's grace in accordance with the principles stated herein and to pass these principles on to future generations so that He will be honored and glorified as our families reflect His character.

The Bible

We believe the Bible was written by men who were divinely inspired by God the Holy Spirit, and we believe it to be authoritative and errorless in its original autographs. We believe the Bible contains the blueprints for building solid marriage and family relationships. It teaches principles for marriage and family life that transcend time and culture. We are committed to communicating biblical truth in order to strengthen and give direction to a marriage and family.

(2 Timothy 3:16; 2 Peter 1:20-21; Hebrews 4:12)

Family

We believe God is the originator of the family. It was established by God in His inaugural act of the marriage between a man and a woman. The Bible further defines the family through God's instruction for married couples to have children, whether by birth or by adoption. We believe the purpose of the family is to glorify and honor God by forming the spiritual, emotional, physical, and economic foundation for individuals, the church, and any society.

It is at home that children see manhood and womanhood modeled. It is at home that moral values are taught by parents and placed into the hearts of their children. It is at home that people see the reality of a relationship with Jesus Christ modeled. It is at home that people learn to live out their convictions. Therefore, we are committed to upholding the concept of family as God's original and primary means of producing a godly offspring and passing on godly values from generation to generation.

(Ephesians 3:14-15; Genesis 1:26-28; Romans 8:15,23; John 1:12; Galatians 3:29; Psalm 78:5-7; Deuteronomy 6:4-9)

Marriage

We believe God, not man, created marriage. We believe marriage was the first institution designed by God. We believe the Bible teaches that the covenant of marriage is sacred and life long. The Bible makes it clear that marriage is a legally binding public declaration of commitment and a private consummation between one man and one woman, never between the same sex. Therefore, we believe God gives a wife to a husband and a husband to a wife, and they are to receive one another as God's unique and personal provision to help meet their mutual needs.

We believe God created marriage for the purpose of couples glorifying God as one flesh, parenting godly children, and enjoying sexual pleasure. As iron sharpens iron, we believe God uses marriage to sharpen a man and woman into the image of Jesus Christ. Just as the Trinity reflects equal worth with differing roles, we believe God created a man and a woman with equal worth but with differing roles and responsibilities in marriage.

Finally, we declare the marriage commitment must be upheld in our culture as that sacred institution of God in which men and women can experience the truest sense of spiritual, emotional, and physical intimacy, so that the two can become one.

(Genesis 2:18-25; Ephesians 5:30-32; 1 Corinthians 7:3; Matthew 19:4-6; Mark 10:6-9; Mark 12:25; Proverbs 27:17; Romans 1:26-27, 8:29; Hebrews 13:4; Matthew 22:30; Deuteronomy 24:5; Song of Solomon)

Husbands

We believe God has charged each husband to fulfill the responsibility of being the "head" (servant leader) of his wife. We believe God created a man incomplete, and as a husband, he needs his wife as his helper. We believe a husband will give account before God for how he has loved, served, and provided for his wife. We reject the notion that a husband is to dominate his wife. Likewise, we reject the notion that a husband is to abdicate his responsibilities to lead his wife. Rather, we believe his responsibility is to love his wife. This love is characterized by taking the initiative to serve her, care for her, and honor her as a gift from God. We believe his responsibility is to protect his wife and help provide for her physical, emotional, and spiritual needs.

We also believe a husband is to seek after and highly regard his wife's opinion and counsel and treat her as the equal partner she is in Christ. Therefore, we are committed to exhort and implore men not to abuse their God-given responsibilities as husbands, but rather to initiate a sacrificial love for their wives, in the same way Jesus Christ initiated sacrificial love and demonstrated it fully on the cross.

(Genesis 2:18-25; Ephesians 5:22-33; Colossians 3:19; 1 Peter 3:7; 1 Timothy 5:8)

Wives

We believe God has charged each wife to fulfill the responsibility of being her husband's "helper." We believe a wife will give account to God for how she has loved, respected, and given support to her husband. We uphold the biblical truth that she is of equal value with her husband before God. We reject the notion that a wife should assume the leadership responsibilities of her husband. Likewise, we reject the notion that a wife should passively defer to the dominance of her husband. We believe that her responsibility is to willingly and intelligently affirm, respect, and submit to her husband as the leader in the relationship and in his vocational calling. Therefore, we are committed to exhorting a wife to be in support of her husband by accepting and excelling in her responsibility as his helper.

(Genesis 2:18-25; Ephesians 5:22-33; Colossians 3:18; 1 Peter 3:1-6; Proverbs 31:10-12)

Sexual Union

We believe the Bible clearly states that marriage is the only context for sexual intimacy. We believe contemporary culture is pressing single people to engage prematurely in acts that are intended only for the context of marriage. Our culture has rejected God's plan for intimacy by promoting sexual promiscuity of various kinds and, as a consequence, has brought upon itself sexual diseases and relational dysfunctions. We believe in sexual purity and fidelity.

Therefore, we are committed to training parents to teach their children at an early age to respect their sexuality and to preserve their virginity and purity until marriage. We are committed to communicating the message to teenagers, single adults, and married couples that sexual intimacy is available only in the context of marriage. (Genesis 1:24-25; Romans 1:24-27; 1 Thessalonians 4:3-8)

Fathers

We believe God has charged a father to execute the responsibilities of a family leader. He is accountable before God to lead his family by sacrificially loving his wife and children and by providing for their physical, spiritual, and emotional needs. We believe the greatest way a father can love his children is to love their mother. We believe children gain much of their concept of God from their fathers. We believe a father should teach his children, by instruction and example, truth from the Bible and how to apply it practically in daily life. Therefore, a father should spend a quantity of time, as well as quality time, with each child.

We believe a father should demonstrate godly character revealed in humility, tenderness, and patience toward his children. We believe a father should demonstrate love by practicing consistent discipline with each child. Therefore, we are committed to turning the hearts of fathers back to their children by emphasizing the importance of their role as "father." We are committed to exhorting every father to model a love for God and His Word, to model love for his wife, and to love his children.

(Malachi 4:6; Ephesians 6:4; Colossians 3:20-21; Deuteronomy 6:4-9; 1 Timothy 3:4-5; 5:8)

Mothers

We believe God has uniquely designed women to be mothers. We believe the greatest way a mother can love her children is to love their father. We also believe God has created a woman with an innate and special ability to nurture and care for her children.

Therefore, we believe mothers are the primary people who execute the vital responsibilities of loving, nurturing, and mentoring children. We believe these responsibilities should be met before a mother contemplates any other duties. We believe our culture has devalued the role of a mother by placing greater significance on activities outside the home than on those inside the home.

We realize there are cases where a mother will find it necessary to work outside the home (e.g. financial distress, single parenthood); however, we also believe some couples have made career and lifestyle choices that result in de-emphasizing the mother's role as nurturer. Therefore, we are committed to presenting a biblical framework through which couples can rightly evaluate their priorities in light of a mother's role. We are committed to elevating motherhood by rightly assessing its exalted value in God's economy of the family. We are committed to exhorting mothers to model love for God and His Word, to model love for her husband, and to love her children.

(Titus 2:4,5; 1 Thessalonians 2:7; Proverbs 14:1, 31:1-31; Deuteronomy 6:6, 11:19; Ezekiel 16:44-45)

Children

We believe children are the gifts of God and should be received and treated as such. We believe a child's life begins at conception. We believe children have a special responsibility to God in obeying and honoring their parents. We believe a child's identity and spiritual growth is either helped or hindered by his parents' devotion to God, to one another, and to him. Parents should see themselves as God's ambassadors, working to build strong character in the lives of their children through consistent godly living, nurturing, discipline, and teaching them right from wrong. We are committed to God's plan for passing His love down through the ages by encouraging parents to love their children "so the generations to come might know" the love and forgiveness of Christ.

(Ephesians 6:1-3; Colossians 3:20; Psalms 78:5-8, 127:3-6, 139:13-16; Proverbs 4:1, 6:20; Job 3:3)

Childless Couples

We believe God has allowed some couples to be without biological children according to His sovereign plan in their lives. We believe couples without children are of no less value before God than those with children. We believe in encouraging childless couples to consider adoption as a family alternative. We are committed to encouraging childless couples to pass on a godly legacy through involvement with children in their immediate families, churches, and communities.

(Luke 1:6-7; Romans 8:28-29)

Grandparents

We believe grandparents are to be honored as valued family members. We believe their wisdom in living should be sought and passed on to their children and their children's children. We also believe that grandparents have the responsibility of teaching and modeling to their grandchildren how to know Jesus Christ and grow in a relationship with Him as well as passing along biblical principles for godly living. The Old Testament is filled with examples of grandfathers and grandmothers who excelled in their roles of grandparenting.

Therefore, we are committed to giving honor to grandparents by encouraging their children and grandchildren to listen to their voices of wisdom. We are also committed to exhorting grandparents to pray for and become actively involved with children and grandchildren whenever it is possible.

(1 Timothy 5:4; Genesis 18:18-19; Proverbs 17:6; Psalm 78)

Church

We believe the family and the church are interdependent. A primary responsibility of the church is to help build godly families, and godly families also help build the church. We believe the family supplies the relational rudiments of the local church. We believe the local church is the spiritual home where families should corporately worship God. It is the place where the knowledge and love of God may be communicated to fathers, mothers, and children.

Therefore, we are committed to exhorting families to support the local church through their involvement. We are also committed to exhorting the local church to uphold the priority of helping build godly marriages and families.

(1 Timothy 3:15; Ephesians 5:22-33; Philemon 1:2; Colossians 4:15)

Divorce

We believe God's plan for marriage is that it be a lifelong commitment between one man and one woman. We believe God hates divorce. We believe divorce brings harm to every person involved. Therefore, reconciliation of a marriage should be encouraged and divorce discouraged. We also believe that God allows for divorce in certain situations, not because He wills it, but because of the hardness of people's hearts. We believe the Bible teaches that God allows for divorce in the case of adultery and in the case where an unbelieving spouse has chosen to abandon the commitment of marriage.

We believe, however, that it is God's priority that marital oneness be restored and that, through the power of the gospel of Jesus Christ, forgiveness and reconciliation be experienced. We believe that in the unfortunate cases of abuse and abandonment, God has provided protection for an abused spouse and provision for child support through the church, civil law, godly counselors, prayer, and other practical measures. We believe God can restore broken people and broken marriages by His grace, by the power of His Spirit, and by His practical truths found in the Bible.

(Malachi 2:16; Matthew 5:31-32; Matthew 19:3-9; Mark 10:6-12; Luke 16:18; Romans 7:1-3; Romans 13:1-5; 1 Corinthians 7:15)

Single Parents

We believe that, ideally, a child needs the influence of both a father and mother for healthy development in life and relationships. At the same time, we recognize that God's grace is sufficient and that He is a father to the fatherless and a husband to the husbandless. We also believe He is a guardian to children without a mother and a friend to a husband who has lost his wife.

We believe God, by His grace, can use the void left from a missing parent to accomplish His eternal purposes of building Christlike character in single parents and their children. We believe a single parent and his or her children are a family and that the Bible contains principles for them to grow as a family. We believe the local church should be a home for single parents, providing their children with godly people who serve as role models in place of the missing parent.

Therefore, we are committed to exhorting Christians within the local church to creatively help meet the needs associated with single-parent homes. We are committed to comforting and encouraging single-parent families by providing resources and developing biblical principles to assist those who struggle in the role of a single parent.

(Psalm 68:5-6; 1 Corinthians 7:32; James 1:27; 1 Timothy 5:3-16; Romans 8:28-29; Luke 18:3-5)

Broken and Blended Families

We believe God has allowed men and women, either by circumstance or by choice, to endure difficult and painful consequences in their marriages and family relationships. We also believe God gives abundant grace to the broken, blended, and single-parent families.

Therefore, we believe He can and does enable them to carry out His functions and principles for healthy family life. We are committed to comforting, encouraging, and teaching these families

God's principles of marriage and family life. We are also committed to exhorting the local church to help with the burden of the broken family.

(James 1:27; 1 Timothy 5:16; Philippians 4:13)

Work and Family

We believe work is an important and necessary aspect of one's service to God and one's responsibility to provide for the needs of the family. We also believe security and significance cannot be found through pursuing career goals or financial achievement apart from one's responsibility to God and one's spouse and family. Instead, we believe those needs are best met in the warmth of a home where parents and children are experiencing harmony in their relationships with each other and with Jesus Christ. Therefore, we are committed to challenging any person or couple to rearrange their priorities so that over the course of a lifetime they can be successful at home and not merely successful in their careers.

(Revelation 3:14-22; Ephesians 6:7-8; Matthew 6:33; 1 Timothy 5:8; 1 Thessalonians 4:10-12)

Mentors

We believe in the biblical admonition for older men and women to teach younger men and women. We believe younger couples today should seek out older couples for their wisdom and counsel in matters of marriage and family. We believe older couples should be taught and encouraged to mentor younger couples and we believe this is best accomplished through the local church. Therefore, we are committed to establishing a strategy for mentoring that the local church may implement and use to build strong marriages and families.

(Titus 2:3-5)

Marriage Education

We believe single adults who choose to marry should be taught the biblical principles of marriage. We also believe the education of a married couple does not end after the wedding ceremony is over, but continues throughout life.

Therefore, we believe that both premarital and postmarital education is helpful and essential in a couple's growth toward and in oneness. We are committed to elevating, establishing, and teaching the precepts of marriage by which single adults can rightly evaluate their relationships and equip themselves for marriage. We are committed to providing the teaching and training necessary to equip married couples to live a lifetime together as one. Finally, we are committed to showing couples how their marriages can be used by God to give others the hope found only in Jesus Christ.

(Titus 2; 1 Timothy 3:16-17; Acts 16:31-34; John 4:53)

The Deceiver and Culture

We believe there is a living Devil who is God's enemy and whose nature and objective is to lie and deceive. We believe the Devil has attacked God's plan for the family from the beginning of man until now. We believe he uses the various aspects of the culture to promote personal independence, distort the differences between men and women, confuse their roles, and elevate personal rights over marital responsibilities. We believe the Devil seeks to persuade people to move away from God's plan for intimacy and oneness and toward isolation and divorce.

(John 8:44; Genesis 3; Isaiah 14:12-14; Ezekiel 28:12-18; 1 Peter 5:8; Ephesians 6:12; 1 John 2:15)

God—the Creator of the Family

Father

We believe in the Fatherhood of God. The title "Father" implies that God is a relational being. The Bible reveals God has four primary relationships as Father: He is the Father of creation, of the nations, of the Lord Jesus Christ, and of all believers. We believe the Bible presents the title "Father" as one of the primary names Christians should use in addressing and relating to God. In doing so, Christians identify themselves as children who belong to the family of God. We are committed to proclaiming and demonstrating this truth about who God is and who we are, so that God will be glorified, and that He might use us to bring others into His family through a personal relationship with His Son.

(John 1:12; Exodus 3:14-15; Ephesians 3:16; Matthew 6:9; Romans 8:15; Acts 17:24-28)

Son

We believe God the Son, fully revealed in the person of Jesus Christ, was God's final sacrifice for the sins of man through the shedding of His blood on the cross and His resurrection from the dead. We believe He is the only way to know God the Father and to experience His plan for marriage and family. We are committed to introducing people to Jesus Christ in order that, by faith, they might personally receive Him, be born into the family of God, receive forgiveness and eternal life, and begin a relationship with God that is essential in marriage and family life.

(John 1:4,12, 17:3; 1 John 2:23-24; Ephesians 2:19-22; Colossians 1:13-18; Hebrews 1:1-4)

Holy Spirit

We believe God the Holy Spirit is the agent and teacher of a godly marriage and family. We believe when Christian couples and their children consistently yield to His control and power, they will experience harmony in their marriages and families. Therefore, we are committed to sharing the ministry of the Holy Spirit with people so they may know God better, make Him known to others, and appropriate His power in fulfilling their duties in marriage and family relationships.

(John 14:26, 15:26, 16:5-15; Ephesians 5:18-21)

Commitment

In recognition of and in full agreement with these biblical principles regarding marriage and the family, I, by the grace of God, commit myself to adhere to, practice, and teach what God has made clear are my responsibilities within His design of marriage and the family.

For more information about FamilyLife
Conferences, resources, and our daily
radio program, "FamilyLife Today,"
call 1-800-333-1433.